PEASANTS in the MODERN WORLD

PEASANTS in the MODERN WORLD

edited by PHILIP K. BOCK

UNIVERSITY OF NEW MEXICO PRESS

Contents

Introduction

The peasant is a rural native whose long established
order of life takes important account of the city.
—Robert Redfield (1953:31)

Most anthropologists would accept the above statement, with various modifications, as a minimal definition of peasantry. Some would wish to limit our consideration to rural agriculturalists, and others would insist that what is important is the peasant's relationship to an elite class, whether or not these social superiors live in an urban center. But Redfield's definition does bring out, in a few words, the essential point about peasants: they exist only in relationship to a larger society of which they form a part.

Anthropologists came to the study of peasant societies after a long period of preoccupation with "primitives," i.e., relatively isolated tribal peoples whose ways of life could be profitably studied with little reference to what went on outside of the local community. In recent years our approach to such primitive groups has changed; we now take fuller account of the social and economic fields in which every human society is included. And this is, in part, a consequence of our involvement in peasant studies, for to study a peasant community as an isolate is to miss the point completely. Anthropologists soon recognized that, again to quote Redfield,

1

the peasant is differently situated from the primitive because peasants know of and are dependent upon more civilized people. There is another dimension of life, outside the village, in that powerful manor or that alarming town. The peasant has given his hostage to the fortunes of a society and mode of life that is both like his and yet alien to it. He keeps the integrity of his traditions by making compromises: by selling his grain in the town, paying his taxes, respecting the priest or the political leader, acknowledging that there are things out there that are perhaps better than his own village. . . . every peasant finds his self-respect, his contentment, qualified by the knowledge that he is poorer and ruder than the gentry, those people of the towns. (1956:74-75)

Historians have been interested in peasant life at least since Carlyle called their attention away from kings and battles to the "kitchens of history." There is a long tradition in Europe of studying the customs and costumes of *das volk*—a tradition which has too often been connected with self-glorifying nationalism and romanticism. But it has been the great political upheavals of the twentieth century and the contemporary concern with underdeveloped nations which have drawn the attention of many social scientists to peasant studies. The masterful study *Social Origins of Dictatorship and Democracy* by Barrington Moore, Jr., illustrates one aspect of this interest, while the many books and articles on economic development in "traditional" societies reflect other concerns (cf. Erasmus 1961; Foster 1962; Steward 1967).

The anthropological contribution to peasant studies consists of both firsthand investigations of contemporary peasant communities and comparative essays dealing with particular regions, topics or institutions. (For an extensive bibliography, see Halpern and Brode 1967.) The original essays presented in this collection are both descriptive and comparative. They illustrate contemporary concerns with new areas and problems as well as continuities of research interests within the field (cf. the excellent collection of previously published articles edited by Potter, Diaz and Foster 1967). Before turning to these contributions, however, I should like to make a few remarks on the nature of peasant society.

Although the majority of the world's population today lives in peasant or peasant-like societies—the greatest concentrations being found in India, China and Latin America—it is generally believed that the peasant way of life is doomed to extinction. In a brief essay, Jack M. Potter points out that both the capitalist and the Communist routes to modernization involve the ulimate destruction of peasantry, almost as a by-product of industrialization. (*in* Potter *et al.* 1967:378-383) Perhaps this is true, and the subsistence-oriented peasant is everywhere destined to be transformed into either a market-oriented farmer or a member of the rural or urban proletariat. But though I am reasonably free of any attachment to the romantic image of peasant life, I want to suggest that the incipient demise of peasant societies—whatever its consequences for individual peasants—may be a very mixed blessing for mankind as a whole, and that the peasant's proverbial conservatism and suspicion of change may play a special role in human history.

The "classic" peasant community exists in a tension between isolation and absorption. The key to its continuity as a community lies in its *relative self-sufficiency*: its products are essential to the (urban) elite class it supports but, even though it is subject to the political and cultural dictates of that elite, it retains a high degree of economic independence. This self-sufficiency may be found on the level of the household, of the village or of the local market community. In any case, what it means is that classic peasantry are less economically dependent on the elite than the elite is on them. Thus, during periods of political unrest or imperial decline, the peasant community has been able to survive. It has faced hardships and losses, to be sure, but it has maintained its integrity as a social group by virtue of containing within itself all the personnel and subsistence skills necessary for survival.

The integration of a peasant community into a state level of organization is always a matter of degree. It is also subject to periodic fluctuations as the fortunes of the state rise and fall, and as the mechanisms of articulation between elite and peasantry change over time. There are, then, two general directions in which a classic peasantry can move in the process of becoming something different. On the one hand, as already noted, it may become absorbed into the state (e.g., through exclusive dependence on cash crops or wage labor), eventually losing the skilled personnel necessary to its integrity. On the other hand, and this is much less frequently recognized, the peasant community may become divorced from its elite and revert to a more "primitive" level of organization.

The Yucatecan village of Tusik, described by Redfield and by Villa R., comes to mind as one familiar example of this process: a peasant community which, in this case, deliberately withdrew from the control of a national state and became "tribalized" (cf. Redfield 1941). The Kachin villages described by E. R. Leach in his *Political Systems of Highland Burma* partly fit this model, as do the Lacandones whose ancestors were very likely peasants in the Pre-Columbian Maya state. Thus, although contemporary research is primarily concerned with the effects of industrialization and market economies upon peasant societies, I think that we must also recognize the potential of such groups to become isolated and tribalized under special circumstances. Indeed, we probably underestimate the frequency with which this has occurred. For example, following the Fall of Rome there were several centuries during which communities on the margins of the Empire were relatively free of state control. The Church provided the only major integrative force in Western Europe during the highly decentralized feudal period; in fact, the political system of feudal Europe departs from the classic type of peasant society in the direction of a loose federation of chiefdoms.

Despite the current popularity of evolutionary thinking in anthropology, I believe that the peasant case bears more similarities to the process of *domestication* (i.e., cultural selection) than it does to natural selection. In general, domestication involves both the usefulness of a given species to its human masters and the dependence of that species upon humans for subsistence and protection. Domesticated varieties of plants frequently lose the ability to propagate themselves without human assistance. Since they would otherwise disappear within one generation, such varieties may be said to have become irrevocably committed to human patronage.

Other varieties, however, and most animal species, retain the ability to revert to a feral way of life, and to reproduce in the wild. This is clearly to their advantage (in terms of survival) should their human protectors cease to find them useful.

In these ways, the classic peasant community may be thought of as semi-domesticated. Its "incomplete" relationship to the elite and its relative self-sufficiency are potentially adaptive in case of disaster. By avoiding total dependence on the state, peasants keep the alternative of autonomy open in case the state should collapse or become overly oppressive.

The essays that follow show peasantry in various degrees of relation to state institutions. In some of them, we see the process of integration advancing quite rapidly. But in several we can detect a peasantry holding the state at arm's length, and seeking a *modus vivendi* which will permit the maintenance of some degree of local autonomy. Given the instability of political relations among today's national states, this attitude may well constitute a kind of "folk wisdom" which has survival value for mankind as a whole.

Eugene Hammel's paper demonstrates, among other points, the adaptive flexibility of family and community organization among Balkan peasants. Here, as in northern Greece, it is primarily kinship (rather than individual patrons or national institutions) which links the village to the urban centers. Hammel provides an ample historical background for understanding the contemporary situation in a part of the world that is relatively unfamiliar to American anthropologists.

Eva and Robert Hunt's article on the rural court in Mexico revolves around the differential use of court facilities by Indian and Mestizo peasants. Several points are made, but I find most interesting the fact that both groups are related to this national institution in a potentially adaptive way: the Indians by holding it "at arm's length" in order to protect their own cultural patterns, and the Mestizos by drawing the representative of the national culture into their own social network. (June Nash's recent paper on the increasing homicide rate in a Mexican Indian community raises some interesting questions in relation to this paper; cf. Nash 1967).

Edward Dozier gives us an overview of the changes wrought in Mexican-American culture by, on the one hand, the isolation of the villages in northern New Mexico and, on the other, the inclusion of Spanish-Americans in rapidly developing urban centers from Texas to California. The changing role of the village, the church, the family and *compadrazgo* relationships are sketched against their Mexican peasant background.

Charles Erasmus compares agrarian reform programs in three Latin-American countries, and it is notable that his analysis is based on firsthand experience in all three areas. Despite the very different starting points in each country, Erasmus shows that land reform without associated developmental programs can do little for a people's standard of living, though it may have other important functions.

Robert Birrell compares the history of agricultural modernization in three nations—England, Japan, and India—to determine the role of certain social institutions in blocking or facilitating processes of change. Like Erasmus, he doubts that land reform by itself can benefit the peasantry, but his method is closer to that of Barrington Moore, Jr., and Gunnar Myrdal. Birrell is particularly interested in Myrdal's thesis that the "parasitic landlord" is a major obstacle to agricultural change in India and he provides interesting comparative materials on this point.

The remaining three papers deal with more general topics. David Burleson surveys the current state of peasant health, outlining demographic and nutritional factors which are essential to understanding the future of peasantry on a worldwide scale. Mary Helms points out that there exist numerous small-scale societies with incomplete relations to a state economy which show few of the characteristics attributed to classic peasantry. These "purchasers," she suggests, share certain distinctive characteristics and should be considered separately in the formulation of social typologies. Finally, Alex Weingrod suggests that our ways of thinking about the relation between "folk" and "elite" cultural traditions need to be reconsidered in the light of the urban explosion and the communications revolution.

Although none of these essays has been previously published, earlier versions of the papers by Alex Weingrod, Mary Helms, and Robert and Eva Hunt were read at the sixty-sixth annual meeting of the American Anthropological Association in Washington, D.C., 1967. In all of these essays we see an effort to test and revise traditional concepts of peasant life. Whether they are doomed or not, the peasant societies of the world provide an important opportunity for anthropology, pure and applied, to test its concepts and broaden its approaches to the manifold complexities of human social life.

Philip K. Bock
The University of New Mexico

CHARLES J. ERASMUS

Agrarian vs Land Reform:
Three Latin-American Countries

It has been my privilege to observe at firsthand the results of agrarian reform programs in three Latin-American countries— Bolivia, Mexico, and Venezuela. The experience has left me with mixed feelings on the subject. While the rural populations of most underdeveloped countries obviously need help, the expropriation and redistribution of land cannot by itself eliminate rural poverty. But the phase "agrarian reform" has come to include much more than we in Anglo-America tend to think of as "land reform." In fact, there is a growing tendency in Latin America to emphasize rural development at the expense of land redistribution, a deliberate policy that reflects an increasing awareness of the limitations and disappointments that attend too narrow a view of rural social problems. In this article I shall frequently make comparisons among the three countries; their problems are similar. But I shall do this in the process of discussing each country in turn, for my focus will be on the special lessons each can teach us about the merits and weaknesses of agrarian reform. Bolivia illustrates the limitations of a program involving little more than the expropriation and redistributon of land. In Mexico, on the other hand, extensive land reform was followed by intensive rural development involving high inputs of capital investment and technological know-how. However, subsequent reconsolidation of land-reform plots into corporately managed farm units has been an unanticipated consequence which largely nullifies the intent of land redistribution. In Venezuela, where land reform has been secondary to technological change and to the development and colonization of new lands, we have the best example of a modern approach to agrarian reform.

Boliva

My study of Bolivia was concentrated in the southeastern departments (states) of Chuquisaca and Tarija. The typical problems of rural Bolivia—high transporation costs, lack of markets and primitive technology—are as severe there as anywhere in the country. Bolivia is ruggedly mountainous with few paved roads, and the dirt highway that connects the southeast with Cochabamba is not negotiable during much of the year. Even if all-weather roads were suddenly provided it would take time for markets to develop. Bolivia's population is overwhelmingly rural, and without accessible export markets most of the agricultural produce gets no farther than the peasant's table. In a year of bumper crops the small urban markets quickly saturate, and prices fall. The peasant finds little opportunity to expand his consumption of manufactured goods through the sale of food surpluses. Geographic and social isolation have resulted in a rural economy that is largely subsistence-oriented.

These very circumstances accounted in large part for the "feudal exploitation" of farm labor against which the 1952 revolution was directed. The large haciendas of southeastern Bolivia gave up two-thirds of their cultivable land in perquisite subsistence plots to serfs in exchange for labor to work the remaining third. Serfs owed their master roughly half the days of the year in free labor to work his fields, build and repair his hacienda house, serve as his domestics, collect his firewood, and sometimes spin his wool and manufacture his *chicha* (corn beer). Even large landowners were limited in the pursuit of wealth by the lack of markets and the difficulties of transportation. They availed themselves of one form of "wealth" made possible through control of the productive land, the human labor which they lavishly and conspicuously consumed in the construction and maintenance of impressive haciendas and in domestic service. To some readers it may seem incredible that a society as feudal as this could have survived as late as the middle of the twentieth century. But similar conditions still exist in parts of Peru and Ecuador.

The Bolivian revolution, and the agrarian reform that followed, gave the serfs the land they had previously held on loan from their hacendados. They no longer owed anyone free labor. In effect the reform simply canceled all "feudal" work obligations and gave the serfs inalienable usufruct of their subsistence plots. As in most cases of land reform, the beneficiaries cannot sell these holdings; the state itself becomes the landowner and sets the conditions of tenure.

North Americans often have the idea that land-reform beneficiaries are radicals with strong Communist leanings. Bolivia demonstrates how mistaken this notion can be. Its rural masses are very resistant to any attempts to organize them into collective farm operations and they jealously defend all inequities in the size of their meagre farm plots. On those large properties, where even the portion cultivated by the hacendados was expropriated, this portion was often converted into a "collective" to be worked by all the ex-serfs in collaboration. In nearly all cases these collectives have been divided up by the ex-serfs with or without official permission. As for the plots given them by the reform, no general attempt was made to equalize them. The same striking inequities in size of plots that existed before 1952 have been perpetuated by the reform. But nowhere did peasants I interviewed favor a more equitable redivision of holdings. The very idea fills most of them with alarm.

These reactions of the Bolivian peasantry are paralleled by land-reform beneficiaries in both Mexico and Venezuela. Collectives in Mexico have been a striking failure. Land-reform beneficiaries are strongly opposed to them but none more strongly than former collective members. Mexican authorities usually relax their pressures to maintain collective farms once members become sufficiently persistent and intransigent in their demands to divide the land into family plots. In Venezuela the government has exerted considerably more pressure to maintain its few collective farms. In the case of collective Cascarí, members finally took matters into their own hands and divided the property among themselves. At others I found the majority of members either verging on revolt or strongly opposed to collective operations.

Inequalities in the size of holding have occurred in many land-reform communities in Venezuela where squatting preceded official expropriation. Venezuelan officials feel these inequities are minor compared with the turmoil that would be created by any attempt at reapportionment. In Mexico, plot sizes are usually uniform within the same *ejido* (land-reform association) but often vary enormously between neighboring *ejidos*. But among all but the most disadvantaged *ejidos,* the suggestion of equalizing holdings meets with vigorous opposition. In attitudes of independence and tenure, land-reform beneficiaries are miniature landlords—not militant Bolsheviks.

Given the social—rather than economic—nature of the Bolivian reform, its effect on rural living standards is precisely what one would expect. The decaying hacienda buildings that dot the countryside are reminders of the quaint and lopsided style of life that so recently and so conspicuously provided a small elite with half the working time of their impoverished serfs. The working time has been returned to this labor force, but since the economic situation remains unchanged there are only limited ways in which the additional time can be used to raise living standards. Many peasants migrate to northern Argentina to earn money during sugarcane harvests. Others invest labor in home improvements of their own by installing paved floors and tile roofs in place of the former dirt and thatch. But so far as increased earning power in agriculture is concerned, the same limitations apply as before.

There is no question that the Bolivian peasants appreciate their release from servitude. In this regard their initial reaction to the reform was not unlike that of the Haitian peasantry after the first great land "reform" in the Western Hemisphere—that which followed the Haitian slave insurrection of 1791.

During the early period of Haitian independence under the leadership of Toussaint, Dessalines and Christophe, French plantations were maintained as state farms on which the former slaves continued to work under a system of controls hardly less strict than those of the slavery from which they had nominally been liberated. But with the fragmentation of the great estates begun by Petion (1807-1818) and continued by Boyer (1818-1843), the Haitian farm economy changed drastically in emphasis from one of markets and exports to one of subsistence. Few of the erstwhile slaves had ever had occasion to taste the fruits of the island's highly profitable plantation economy. As consumers they had never acquired the incentives necessary for intensive market production.

Similarly, in Bolivia for a brief time after the 1952 revolution there was a decrease in market produce which created inflationary food prices in the cities. In enjoyment of their new freedom, the peasants concentrated on their own needs while many of the hacendados who had been producing for the urban markets fled temporarily to the cities or abandoned their farms forever. During this period when urban living was most austere many of the professionally trained members of the middle class left Bolivia for jobs in Chile, Peru, and Venezuela. But today Bolivian peasants are satisfying the urban markets and willingly increase their market production when they have the opportunity. They want more radios, bicycles, sewing machines and other manufactured goods of which there are still very few in most rural areas. The pre-reform Bolivian peasants of the mid-twentieth century were far more market-oriented than the newly liberated Haitian slaves of the early nineteenth.

The Bolivian countryside is now ready for an economic revolution, but that will require enormous amounts of capital investment. That land redistribution by itself cannot effect an economic revolution is now admitted by Bolivians. However, some officials are still so much on the defensive about land reform that they deride purely economic appraisals of it as "materialistic" and insist the true measure of its success is "social." Considering the conditions of serfdom that existed in Bolivia before 1952, the point they are making is certainly not a trivial one. But will these social effects be progressive without economic and technological growth?

MEXICO

Mexico has made impressive investments in rural development, particularly in the northwest. In an area that twenty years ago did not even have a paved road connecting it with the capital or the U.S. border, the federal government has invested heavily in dams, irrigation, paved highways and public power. The investments have certainly transformed northwestern Mexico, as anyone knows who has watched the remarkable changes that have transpired in Sonora and Sinaloa since World War II. Although not called "agrarian reform" when they began, these capital investments are today considered an integral part of a balanced agrarian reform program. Mexicans no longer expect land redistribution to raise rural living standards.

The most interesting aspect of the Mexican case is the management problem that arises when land-reform beneficiaries are further benefited by extensive capital improvements. The irrigation districts in the Yaqui and Mayo river valleys of southern Sonora illustrate this problem. In the old days farmers flood-irrigated their land with water provided by the annual inundations of the rivers. Seed was saved from the last harvest, and plowing and cultivating were done with draft animals pastured in adjoining thorn forests. Development of the irrigation districts has greatly extended the area of cultivation and with it the farming population. But now not only is the water taxed, but commercial crop seeds, fertilizers and insecticides have all become increasingly necessary. Moreover, opening the thorn forest to more farm land has left no place to pasture draft animals. Although machinery is available, most farmers cannot afford to own their own; they either rent equipment or contract their plowing and harvesting.

Thus, even for the smallest landowner or land-reform beneficiary, farming must now be financed. The Ejido Bank, which was established to provide land-reform beneficiaries with farm credit, has funds sufficient to help less than a fourth of the land-reform beneficiaries in the Yaqui and Mayo River Irrigation Districts. The rest are forced to rent or sharecrop (the tenant provides the financing and the land-reform beneficiary the land).

According to the Mexican agrarian code, which establishes the conditions of tenure for land-reform beneficiaries, neither renting nor sharecropping of *ejido* plots is permissible. In all three countries the land-reform laws promote personal management of the properties distributed to beneficiaries and discourage their reconsolidation or fragmentation by sale, renting, sharecropping, marriage or inheritance. But the restrictions on renting and sharecropping have long been openly violated throughout Mexico. Recently, when the director of the Ejido Bank for the state of Sonora brought a civil suit against men renting large acreages of *ejido* land within the Yaqui River Irrigation District, the state supreme court refused to hear the case. For all practical purposes this action by the court has now legalized the practice.

Land renting is done by some entrepreneurial farmers on a large scale. Using their own farm machinery they rent large blocks of contiguous *ejido* plots that can be plowed, crop dusted and harvested as a unit. For the same reasons sharecroppers find it more economical to work adjoining parcels, and even the Ejido Bank endeavors to work with groups of adjoining land-reform beneficiaries rather than with scattered individuals. The Bank stipulates the crops to be planted, manages the farming operations and employs land-reform beneficiaries only at manual tasks, mainly during irrigation. These manual labor requirements represent less than ten per cent of the total cropping costs. In such a situation, land-reform beneficiaries working with the Bank are little different from those working with an entrepreneur on a sharecropping basis. They are simply shareholders in a financial venture managed by someone else.

This tendency for redistributed lands to reconsolidate for management purposes when capitalization takes place is strongest in

Mexico. In Bolivia, where capitalization of agriculture has been minimal, I observed no cases at all. In Venezuela, in 1964, the sharecropping form was rare but seemed to be spreading.

In Mexico, as in Bolivia, it is difficult to see how land redistribution has lifted material living standards. The relative prosperity of land-reform beneficiaries depends upon the size of their holdings and upon the extent of rural capitalization by the government in their area. For the majority of beneficiaries the holdings are too small to provide anything but a minimal standard of living. In Sonora well over three-fourths must seek supplementary income during the year, usually as field hands and occasionally as unskilled or semiskilled construction laborers in the rapidly growing urban areas. It is the overall economic expansion of this region due to government irrigation and road-building projects that has been most influential in raising living standards. There are more opportunities than ever for small farmers and land-reform beneficiaries to find seasonal and part-time employment to supplement their meagre farm incomes. The rising prosperity of the area has also affected the attitudes of merchants toward consumer credit. Rural households find it increasingly easy to buy bicycles, radios and home furnishings with small down payments and no collateral. The pressure of time payments is often an additional incentive to seek part-time employment off the farm.

Many land-reform beneficiaries within the irrigation districts, particularly the Indians, would prefer to plant subsistence crops. They complain of the loss of freedom which has followed the irrigation developments. Forced to seek credit from the Ejido Bank or from sharecroppers to meet the expenses of planting, they become obligated to plant commercial crops such as cotton. Others simply rent their parcels and seek wage labor where they can find it. While all of this is unpleasant to the subsistence-oriented peasant, it has had the effect of forcing him more and more into the market and into a widening sphere of commercial relationships. Outside the irrigation zones many land-reform beneficiaries have changed from subsistence to commercial crops on their own. Sesame seed, for example, does much better under local dry-farming conditions than the traditional food crops. Small farmers have been quick to appreciate the fact that the sesame harvested from their small plots will buy them more corn and beans than they could produce themselves. But the marketing possibilities for commercial crops such as sesame are the result of the overall economic development of the area with the attendant intensification of merchandizing.

The question that comes to mind in considering the Mexican case is whether any purpose is served by making land-reform beneficiaries the nominal, lower-class owners of highly capitalized farm operations which are financed, managed and even worked by other persons. When I suggest to a Mexican official that the land redistribution aspects of Mexico's agrarian reform may already have become an anachronism (to provoke an expression of his attitudes), I usually get a very negative response, and sometimes an angry one. But once the official is reassured that I am just as sincerely concerned with the problems and as perplexed by them as he is, he frequently admits that the time will probably come when Mexico will give land-reform beneficiaries negotiable titles to their plots. However, most informed Mexicans with whom I have discussed this problem do not feel the country is ready for such a drastic move.

On occasion I have suggested that the consequences of such a move would not be as drastic as many people expect. Making *ejido* lands a commodity once again would not have to result in pre-revolutionary *latifundismo* (condition of giant land holdings) as long as the present restrictions on maximum farm sizes are retained. For example, in areas of prime land like those in the irrigation districts, one hundred hectares (a little under the average size of U.S. farms) is the most that one person can legally own. Granted that the most able farmers would soon gobble up the rest, this would only mean that for every one who expanded up to this limit, about four or five would eventually be bought out. All farms would then be large enough to afford their owners a middle-class standard of living; the number of competent farm managers necessary to meet the demands of this limit would be a more realistic national goal than the number necessary to make the present *minifundismo* (condition of small land holdings) operate according to land reform ideology; and finally, the less able managers who sold their holdings would simply go on earning their living as wage laborers as they are already doing.

But to these arguments my Mexican friends reply that the results of such a policy would indeed be drastic. Already people get around the laws restricting the size of individual holdings by buying land in the name of relatives or trusted employees. And many renters now farm thousands of acres of *ejido* lands. Making *ejido* land negotiable would so defeat the ideology of Mexico's agrarian reform that there would be no way left of preserving the existing machinery for helping the rural masses.

In the case of Mexico we come back to the same basic problem we encountered in Bolivia. Land redistribution by itself does not result in material, economic improvements for disadvantaged rural populations. But it has social consequences that seem important. The problem is to determine just how important and beneficial these social consequences really are. Unfortunately, our third case, Venezuela, does not provide any final answers, but its own special circumstances add further dimensions to our question.

VENEZUELA

Compared to Mexico and Bolivia, expropriation and redistribution of land is not a major emphasis of agrarian reform in Venezuela. In Mexico about forty-five per cent of all cultivated land is now in the possession of *ejidatarios* (land-reform beneficiaries), and between two-thirds and three-fourths of Bolivia's cultivated land has nominally changed hands since the revolution. Venezuela's land reform, however, has affected less than six per cent of her cultivated lands. While it is true that the Venezuelan experiment is much younger than the other two, the approach to land expropriation in Venezuela has been much more conservative and cautious. For one thing, the owners of expropriated haciendas in Venezuela are so well reimbursed that more land has been offered for expropriation than the government can afford to buy or could find peasants to occupy even if it did. This is very different from Bolivia where many former landowners are now so destitute that few people in the highlands today are willing to risk capital in the purchase or improvement of agricultural land. In Venezuela the public's confidence in its government's respect for private property is so high that in many newly colonized areas farmers are making heavy investments of labor and capital (dairies, orchards, farm buildings) prior to receiving legal title to their land. In Mexico the farmer-entrepreneur's confidence in his ability to circumvent the law is so great that he often makes expensive improvements on land owned illegally.

Venezuela's agrarian reform has three separate aspects of which land reform is only one. The dominant trend in Venezuela, and one certainly reflected in the attitudes or public officials and high-ranking members of the peasant federations, has been to emphasize the other two aspects—the development of new lands and the "consolidation" of agrarian settlements already established. Unlike Bolivia, where colonization and development of new lands in the tropical lowlands is viewed by government personnel as an alternative or supplement to agrarian reform, Venezuelan officials consider it an integral part of their program. With few exceptions, people employed by government agencies active in agrarian reform favor development of new lands rather than purchase and redistribution of those in production. It is a common opinion that money spent in buying farms would be better invested in roads, irrigation works, and land-clearing projects, etc. Many also feel that *planned* colonization is inadvisable. Peasant families quickly move into areas opened up by roads, and a "natural" selection of colonists results. These are usually better prepared psychologically to overcome new hardships than those chosen by planners.

Venezuela's approach to rural development maximizes new opportunities while leaving for later those problems for which there is no ready solution as yet. The western highlands of Venezuela have a dense and very conservative population with serious social and economic problems. In this region one still encounters archaic haciendas on which tenants equipped with oxen and wooden plows produce for absentee landlords under feudalistic forms of administration. Such haciendas are not expropriated because the land is too steep to meet the standards of the Venezuelan Agrarian Institute. Rather than convert marginal lands of this kind into permanent small plots, government policy is to entice the highland population into the lowlands by creating new opportunities there. As rural productivity and prosperity increase in these lowland areas, the nation can then turn to the solution of agricultural problems that involve the greatest social manipulation. It may then be feasible to take farms on eroded marginal lands completely out of cultivation and plant them to forests or pasture.

The third aspect of Venezuela's agrarian reform, "consolidation," refers to the construction of roads, rural housing, irrigation developments, public power and water distribution systems, as well as the facilitation of farm credit, farm machinery, agricultural extension and adult education programs. These projects are intended to insure the success of settlements formed by land redistribution or colonization. Bolivia has been able to afford very few such programs and even those have been heavily subsidized by United States foreign aid. Mexico, as we have seen, has given extraordinary attention to most of these projects but only recently has begun to advertise them as an integral part of agrarian reform. The income from Venezuela's vast oil deposits has provided her with an unusual opportunity to finance a very investment-conscious form of rural development.

The effects of Venezuela's efforts are evident throughout the countryside. The quantity of expensive consumer goods in rural homes is impressive. Refrigerators, for example, have become relatively common in communities with electricity, but the frequency with which one encounters kerosene refrigerators in remote villages is even more remarkable. Radios are common everywhere and bicycles are numerous in settlements near cities and paved highways.

In Venezuela, as in Bolivia and Mexico, greater personal freedom was frequently mentioned by peasants as a highly desirable result of agrarian reform. To work for oneself and to be the "owner of one's work" was considered far superior to sharecropping for another. But in Venezuela, far more than in the other two countries, peasants associated many material benefits directly with agrarian reform. Among those listed were absence of rent payments, availability of credit, farm machinery, rural housing, water, electricity, rural schools, and the all-important roads to market. Many were buying goods they said they had not even hoped to own before: radios, television sets, furniture, better clothes and a more varied and abundant diet. Children were attending school regularly now that their parents no longer had any reason to be ashamed of their apparel. No Venezuelan government in their memory had ever done so much for "los campesinos" (the peasants).

More striking even than the material evidences of rising living standards has been the effect of Venezuela's development policies on the structure of its rural population. The opening of new lands in the lowland interiors has resulted in considerable population movement. For example, settlements and towns in the progressive states of Portuguesa and Barinas contain families from nearly all parts of the nation. When I had occasion to check, I always found the proportion of out-of-state families greater than that of native born. The results of these population movements are reflected in the dramatic contrast between these dynamic, progressive areas and the static western highlands. Families torn from their old kinship and patron-client relationships form new commercial and political associations. Farmer associations, dairy associations, and credit unions, for example, become the vehicles for more active participation by rural interest groups in their own regional development and in the formation of national policy.

Bringing new lands under cultivation through the development of irrigation projects has had similar population effects in northwest Mexico. I met many families that had moved to Sonora from states farther south because they viewed Sonora as a frontier where they could increase their chances for success. While most find it hard to get land, many have initiated commercial enterprises that have done well. A developing area tends to attract the risk-takers or potential entrepreneurs who have found their own habitat too full of frustration. Here again, these spatially mobile families are much more progressive and much more prone to form new commercial and political associations than the more static, native population.

Even in Bolivia the most progressive and dynamic area is that being colonized around Santa Cruz in the eastern lowlands. Much more typical of Bolivia, however, is the static rural situation where land reform has changed the social order in ways that often seem more nominal than real. Land-reform beneficiaries have been organized into peasant syndicates that correspond to former hacienda boundaries except where serfs of two or more small haciendas form one syndicate. On those haciendas where the *patrón* was allowed to retain a portion of the land, he still lives in the hacienda manor. The ex-serfs still tip their hats to him, still call him "patrón" and often work on his reduced holdings as sharecroppers. The traditional rural social structure of Bolivia often seems remarkably resilient despite its political revolution.

Mexican land-reform associations (*ejidos*) seldom preserve pre-reform hacienda work forces. Not only are an *ejido's* lands frequently scattered but the *ejidatarios* themselves may reside in two or more villages. By cutting across community and ethnic (Indian versus Mestizo) lines, *ejidos* have helped to break down traditional social groupings in rural areas.

In Venezuela many haciendas purchased by the Agrarian Institute have been turned over to a peasant syndicate made up of the original work-force, as was so commonly done in Bolivia. These products of Venezuela's agrarian reform are the most unchanged. At such collectives as La Unión, Loro Pedernales and El Rodeo, peasants felt the government had become a new *patrón* while everything else stayed much the same. Where land in the highlands had been divided among the beneficiaries in individual plots, the situation closely resembled the expropriation of a Bolivian *latifundio*. Peasants were cropping in a subsistence-oriented fashion or farming for market to maintain their minimal living standards. Family and neighborhood relationships remained intact, and where peasants had not actually withdrawn from the syndicates, their participation was poor. The dramatic improvements in Venezuela's rural living standards already referred to were mainly among the beneficiaries of redistributed and newly opened land in the lowlands near highways and cities. Here one can find many prosperous farmers who were *conuqueros* (slash-and-burn subsistence farmers) only a few years ago. It is in these areas that family heads are most active in peasant syndicates or farmer associations.

Although different in history and emphasis from the agrarian reforms of Bolivia and Mexico, that of Venezuela confirms the major conclusion to be drawn from our comparison. Rural development that accents capital investments and technological improvements is far more likely to produce a significant rise in rural living standards than is land redistribution. Yet there are many Venezuelans, as there are many Bolivians and Mexicans, who believe land redistribution is a necessary part of agrarian reform for social reasons often labeled the "social function" of land reform. These reasons essentially boil down to the reduction of political tensions through a more equitable distribution of political influence. We shall now consider this social problem.

REDISTRIBUTION OF POLITICAL INFLUENCE

The Haitian case is again useful for comparison because the French period preceding independence was an example of unrestrained coercive power. The Negro farm labor that made possible France's lucrative colonial plantations was slave labor. However, the transformation of slaves into subsistence-oriented peasants did not prevent the usurpation of dictatorial powers by heads of state. Haitian history provides clear testimony to the fact that land redistribution does not insure "democracy" as we know it.

The revolution that deposed the French colonial landowners did not immediately change the system of agricultural production. The early Haitian heads of state maintained forced labor through a system of district agricultural inspectors backed by the army. But once the fragmentation of holdings had begun under Petion it became impossible to stop. When Boyer early in his administration attempted to reinstate a forced labor system in his Rural Code of 1826, he was completely unable to enforce it. Today, when Bolivian peasants claim that no change of government could succeed in taking back the land given them or in remaking them into hacienda peons, they are probably right. Moreover, when they say they have gained greater self-respect and "dignity" with their freedom, the Haitian case substantiates this claim as well. Haitian peasants are fiercely independent, and their personality and demeanor have little in common with "Black Sambo" or "Uncle Tom" stereotypes. Despite all the "Papa Docs" of Haitian history, Haitians act more like Sidney Poitier than Stepin Fetchet. But the freedom of the Haitian peasant is the freedom of poverty, hunger, high infant mortality and a short life-span. Slaves and serfs gain considerable "freedom" and self-respect through land redistribution despite few improvements in living standards and despite the concentration of considerable coercive power in urban areas. The greater "freedom" of the post-1952 Bolivian peasant is no guarantee that Bolivia is now immune to coercive or despotic governments.

Elias T. Tuma, in his important book, *Twenty-six Centuries of Agrarian Reform* (1965), compares several important land-tenure reforms from ancient to modern times. One of his major conclusions is that such reforms are more likely to serve the political goals of reformers than the economic and social needs of the people. Certainly the cases examined here confirm the results of Tuma's historical analysis.

The feudal character of Venezuela's haciendas ended with the close of the Gómez dictatorship in 1935. But land-tenure reform did not begin until after the fall of Pérez Jiménez twenty-five years later. It is true that in many parts of Venezuela, during the rule of Pérez Jiménez, squatters were moved off lands owned by the dictator's henchmen. While some token payment was made to the squatters for their "improvements," it was rarely adequate. Upon the downfall of Jiménez the dispossessed peasants rushed back to reclaim their lands. These numerous property "invasions" throughout Venezuela in the early days of the reform led to an exaggerated view of the "social pressure" for land redistribution. Early estimates of the numbers of land-hungry peasants ranged from 300,000 to 500,000 families. But four years after the agararian reform was initiated only 100,000 families had petitioned for land.

In Mexico, the revolution of 1910 terminated the dictatorship of Porfirio Díaz and led to peasant land invasions in the southern part of the country and to the reform law of 1915. However, large-scale expropriation and redistribution of lands did not really begin until the presidency of Lázaro Cárdenas twenty years later. Cárdenas' desire to strengthen his political influence against that of former president Calles was undoubtedly an important factor in his decision, for he was faced with no widespread urgency to reinterpret the agrarian law.

Bolivia is one case in which land-tenure reform was an integral part of a revolution. Even in Haiti, forced labor on large estates outlasted the slave revolt by more than a generation. However, Bolivia is not really an exceptional case in the sense that social pressures for land reform were general in the countryside at the time it was carried out. Many peasants had to be persuaded and fears of retaliation by the landowners had to be allayed. The southestern sector was influenced by leadership from outside the area. Cochabamba is believed by some to have been one major point from which revolt spread, and the mining state of Potosí may have been another. Two of the most powerful syndicate leaders in the state of Chuquisaca during the early days of the reform were miners from Potosí.

Organization of the Bolivian peasantry into peasant syndicates became the procedure for initiating the expropriation of hacienda land and simultaneously the means of consolidating the rural masses behind the revolutionary party. Once the formation of peasant syndicates had been justified and implemented through land reform, the party in power could use them at election time to amass the show of votes with which it legitimized its authority.

Many of the characteristics and problems of the peasant federations of Bolivia, Mexico and Venezuela parallel those of incipient trade union movements in underdeveloped countries. In the first place they are primarily political organizations. Bruce Millen in his study *The Political Role of Labor in Developing Countries* (1963) calls this characteristic "political unionism" to distinguish it from the collective bargaining orientation of U.S. labor unions. Peasant federations are even less likely to involve the collective bargaining aspects of unionism than are trade unions. The self-employed beneficiaries of land reform can bargain only with their government. The leadership of both trade and peasant syndicates tends to come from a worker or rural "elite" made up of individuals who are better educated, more ambitious, and more experienced in coping with the larger world than is the average worker or peasant. Since dues in both cases are hard to collect, the unions cannot afford full-time officers without government subsidy. Dependence on outside sources for funds often leads to the compromising of principles and even to corruption.

Despite all their inadequacies and despite the tendency for a ruling party to use them as vehicles for the exercise of power, trade unions and peasant federations provide a vital channel of communication between the masses and the political elites of developing countries. Moreover, the attention and importance that political elites ascribe to these structures as vote-buying mechanisms for the legitimation of their authority does, in effect, transfer political influence to the masses. However, it takes a broader agrarian reform program than land redistribution to maintain peasant unions as vote-buying mechanisms. In this regard Venezuela's peasant federation has undoubtedly consigned more political influence to the rural sector than Bolivia's has been able to do. Because of the Venezuelan emphasis on "consolidation" through programs of farm credit, housing, road building, machinery, etc., local peasant leaders are provided with many goals for rural improvements to which they can redirect their political activities after their request for land has been met. And the more local improvements the rural masses obtain by such measures the more they expect their votes and political support to win them in the future. In short, true redistribution of political influence in the rural sector tends to be associated with the economic and technological developments that progressively lift standards and aspirations—not with land redistribution per se.

In underdeveloped countries where most jobs must be filled from a labor market made up of illiterate, unskilled workers, trade unions emphasizing collective bargaining rather than politics are not likely to develop much power to bargain with. One unskilled worker can so easily replace another that stable, unified union memberships are hard to achieve. Unskilled farm laborers have been the last to successfully organize in the United States, and it is precisely among them that the political overtones of membership are far stronger than in most U.S. unions. This situation not only helps us understand why incipient union movements in such countries must be political, it also illustrates why general economic and industrial development is essential to a permanent and broad distribution of political influence. It is only this kind of development that leads to a permanent diversification of the occupational structure among skilled workers and trained specialists. And it is the diversification of labor skills and labor needs that gives each occupational group its bargaining power vis-a-vis the rest. It becomes harder for any one interest group to control all the rest as it becomes more difficult for each to master all the knowledge and skills of the rest.

Industrialization is the most direct path to the diversification of the occupational structure, including the absorption of farm-labor surpluses created by the mechanization of agriculture. But a country with a class system dominated by a landholding aristocracy is one particularly resistant to the kind of entrepreneurial changes that effect industrialization. Thus land redistribution is viewed as necessary in such situations to destroy the older status-quo ideology. Power taken from the conservative aristocracy is thereby made available to a larger sector of the population. But making political influence available to a target sector does not insure its transfer. Illiterate rural populations, unaccustomed to participation in those kinds of voluntary associations that operationalize political influence, are unlikely to absorb all that is made available to them by a drastic land reform; the surplus is eagerly appropriated by a new elite. Bolivia is a case in point.

When I began my stay in Bolivia I was surprised at being gently reprimanded on several occasions by government officials for using the word "Indian." Instead of "indio" I was instructed to speak of "campesinos" (peasants). The word "indio" was regarded as a term of opprobrium applied by the former landed aristocracy to their peons and therefore a symbol of peonage and inferiority. I was very much impressed by this evidence of an ideological change produced by land reform. Not only did officials and employees of the various government bureaucracies refer to the rural population as "campesinos," they greeted all peasants in direct address as "compañero" (comrade). But despite the impressiveness of this deliberate and practiced alteration of vocabularly, the behavior of the officials employing it often contained a patronizing quality that mitigated the ideological intention. When a peasant, dressed in traditional Indian garb, visited a government office, he was generally treated in a conspicuously egalitarian fashion by a bureaucrat dressed in modern garb. No one observing the egalitarian ritual with which the official embraced his country "comrade" would have had difficulty recognizing which of the two was higher in status. But when a *campesino* and a bureaucrat of higher status were dressed alike, some form of protocol was invariably invoked to make the distinction obvious.

For example, whenever officials travel about the countryside in their pickup trucks they are driven by a "chauffeur" who also serves as mechanic if the car breaks down. Unless the chauffeur has recently soiled his clothes and hands in his role as mechanic, he may be indistinguishable from the higher-status official. Although of *campesino* origins, he may not even differ noticeably in skin color. But when these two individuals, who have been riding side by side all day, stop at a village cafe to eat, the official sits at a separate table. It is soon made clear by manner and conversation which of the two is the official. Physical separation announces the status difference, and subsequent behavior explains who is in charge and who is subservient. Comradeship ends at the crucial point where it might really compromise higher status.

One might argue that this conscious change in vocabulary has been largely nominal since many of the behavioral distinctions between *patron* and *peón* remain. This point of view is verbalized even by some peasants when they claim the former *rosca* (landed aristocracy—literally "the screw") has been replaced by a *nueva rosca* (the new bureaucratic elite). There would almost seem to be a contradiction here between this recognition of a *nueva rosca* and the peasants' greater sense of self-esteem, noted previously, which they attribute to the reform. But this very contradiction epitomizes the strength and weakness of land reform as an instrument for redistribution of political influence. The peasant has indeed gained greater independence. He can feel the difference and so can the old aristocracy, which complains incessantly of peasant irresponsibilities that at times approach outright sabotage. But the effect is not cumulative as in those parts of Mexico and Venezuela where intensive capitalization of the rural sector has promoted rising living standards. As people grow accustomed to "progress," they expect more and demand more. Distributing small plots of land to peasants may only enhance their freedom to withdraw further from the contest for influence. They have to aspire to something more than a minimal existence.

None of this means that the ideology of land redistribution is meaningless or unimportant. It involves a healthy concern with standards of social justice. In Mexico and Venezuela the number of technicians employed in rural development prgorams is steadily increasing, as is their dedication and skill. In Mexico, particularly, a great change has taken place in government personnel over the past twenty years. The desire to use an official post as a means of acquiring through graft the capital to start a business or farming venture seems to be much less in vogue. Many able men are making government service a career and taking pride in their reputation for honesty and efficiency. There is a greater tendency today to talk about graft in the past tense. The growing number of skilled and dedicated civil servants has been made possible by the expanding Mexican economy. Land reform has played its part by helping to provide and maintain the justification for rural development. If most of the land in a river valley is owned by a few families, costly irrigation developments by government are much harder to justify in terms of the new social ethic than when those same lands have been redistributed to thousands of poor families. The ideology that accompanies land redistribution can be a much greater catalyst to rural development than the redistribution itself if a country has the resources to follow it up with modern agrarian reform.

CONCLUSIONS

The phrase "agrarian reform" in its broadest sense includes both land redistribution and capital development of the rural sector. I have chosen to contrast these two aspects of planned rural change through a discussion of three national programs I have personally observed. I have come to the following tentative conclusions.

1. Land-tenure reform by itself does not lead to cumulative rural changes. It can give members of a rural population a sense of greater personal freedom and self-respect. It helps provide an ideology critical of asymmetrical standards of social justice, and it helps justify investments in the rural sector that do have cumulative effects.

2. Beneficiaries of land reform tend to be politically conservative rather than politically radical. But this does not mean that land redistributions insure "democracy." Since land reform is more likely to be the product of a politically active "elite" than of a "grassroots" peasant movement, beneficiaries are not simultaneously provided with the knowledge, experience and aspirations to help them consolidate their political influence.

3. When capitalization of the rural sector follows land redistribution, reconsolidation of holdings will tend to take place through corporate management. This follows because modern mechanized agriculture is not economically feasible on tiny farm units and

because competent farm managers are not created by fiat. Problems of credit and management will lead government—in the interest of national productivity—to manage the redistributed lands through one of its own agencies or to permit financing and management by private entrepreneurs. In either case the spirit and the letter of the land-reform code may be deliberately disregarded.

4. Agrarian reform programs that increase the spatial mobility of rural populations, as through the development of new lands, will help to break down traditional forms of social structure and make way for the kind of interest-group associations that effect a wider distribution of political influence in the rural sector.

5. Agrarian reform programs that emphasize capitalization of the rural sector will benefit private farmers as well as land reform beneficiaries. Rural families are more likely to identify with "progress" and begin to link new aspirations with new forms of political participation. In this situation, peasant federations formed by land reform redirect their goals toward other types of rural development as their political experience and influence increase. As broad rural development becomes more and more a national goal, political parties and affiliated associations compete in promoting that goal in order to win the support.

ROBERT BIRRELL

Obstacles to Development in Peasant Societies: An Analysis of India, England, & Japan

INTRODUCTION

In many Asian countries, agriculture is lagging badly in terms of the production and productivity increases expected of it in the early 1950's. Concern as to why this is the case has stimulated a mounting body of research, the results of which are beginning to pay off in terms of some sophisticated theoretical analyses. This paper focuses on the extent to which certain social institutions in contemporary India have impeded agricultural progress in that country. Comparative materials will be drawn from the experience of two societies, England and Japan, which in their separate ways have managed successfuly to modernize their agriculture.

The main theoretical ideas to be discussed here have been taken from the recent work of Gunnar Mydral (1968). Myrdal has summed up much of the thinking of many institutionally oriented analysts of the subject, and has presented extensive yet sharp and persuasive arguments that are likely to be the starting point of much subsequent analysis. The key proposition to be examined is that, so long as Indian agriculture is dominated by the parasitic landlord letting out his land in small lots to tenant households, the prospects for agricultural growth are dim. I will also discuss some alternative theories as to the effects of other social institutions on agricultural development in Asia. In general, I think the analysis supports Mydral's thesis, though it also indicates that parasitic landlordism is itself caused by a complex of economic, social, political, and ecological variables, which must be taken into account by any adequate theory of agricultural development.

INDIA

Prior to the nineteenth century, Indian agriculture was largely carried on by small holders at a subsistence level. Since the major scarcity was not land but men to cultivate it, such social differentiation as existed in the rural areas was based primarily on political factors. The local elite was composed of those who had the power to extract taxes or other forms of tribute from the peasants. Market forces as yet had very little influence on the allocation of goods and services.

Like rural societies elsewhere in Asia, Indian rural society became subject to a variety of forces which fundamentally changed it. The most important of these have been population increases, the spreading of market pressures into village life, and political changes, especially those following the advent of Western imperialism. Let us examine the impact of these forces and the consequences of the institutional adaptions to them.

In India, partly as a consequence of law and order instituted by the British during the nineteenth century, the population expanded rapidly (doubling between 1800 and 1871), and began to encroach on the available land. This process accelerated during the twentieth century, as the population increased from 286 million in 1901 to 438 million in 1951 (Myrdal 1968: 1394-5). The effect of this rapid growth was obviously to reduce the amount of land available per household. By the second half of the nineteenth century new land had become scarce, and little relief from the population pressure was attained through out-migration. With greater land fragmentation, the household's livelihood became increasingly vulnerable to any form of crisis, and the peasant was forced to seek help from sources outside the family. (I am assuming here that the peasant family will only give up its land with the greatest reluctance since to do so is both to give up its major form of security and usually any claim to prestige in the community.)

The ways this vulnerability may be taken advantage of are largely determined by the commercialization of agriculture and by political developments. In India during the nineteenth century there was a considerable increase in rural commerce (Myrdal 1968: 1040-1). At the same time the British introduced concepts of property whereby land became a legally alienable commodity and contracts for it were enforced in the courts. The exposure to commercial agriculture and the wider market system with its new and attractive products carried with it many hazards for the peasant. To the extent that he produced for the market he became dependent on a price system he could not control; moreover, he may have found it necessary to purchase fertilizer and improved seeds for these crops. Finally, he tended to develop new tastes for consumer goods which he did not produce himself. All this occurred just at the time when his diminishing holding had increased his vulnerability. He was therefore often forced to seek credit from the moneylender, and once he did so he usually found it impossible to extricate himself from debt since the high interest he paid added to the financial burden. The result, as amply documented in India (Moore 1966:359-360), was that he had to sell his land; if he refused, his creditors simply foreclosed—a process facilitated by the British legal system. The British also helped accentuate the process in some of their nineteenth century tax settlements, by granting the Zamindars (tax intermediaries) rights of ownership of the land taxed (Moore 1966: 345-7). Subsequent efforts by the British to protect the right of small holders and tenants do not appear to have had much influence.

In India, those who accumulated land in excess of what they could cultivate themselves have in most cases tenanted their land to other peasant households. They have done this partly to avoid the supervisory work necessary to cultivating a large holding with hired labor, and partly because of community pressures to let their

land in small parcels to the landless within the village, but especially because competition among prospective tenants to gain access
to a plot large enough for subsistence ensures a high rent. It also
seems that the economic gains from consolidation are limited,
especially in regard to paddy cultivation where few economies of
scales have been possible. The paddy field tends to be relatively
small due to problems of water control and the necessity of having
a level surface. Moreover, paddy is responsive to increased inputs
of labor such as careful water control procedures and more intensive, repeated cultivation (Geertz 1963: 28-37). Thus by forcing the
small tenant to use his labor extravagantly (in the sense that he
must compete with other peasants for the use of the land) there
seems to be no great gain to be had from letting the land in large
farms to fewer tenants.

In India by the 1950's some ⅓ to ½ of the cultivated land was
tenanted in the form of tiny plots barely large enough to provide
subsistence for the tenant after rent payments (Myrdal 1968:
1055-9). The process of economic differentiation has also created an
even more deprived class of landless laborers, i.e. peasants who
neither own nor tenant land. Figures for the size of this class are
difficult to establish since some peasants who work for wages also
own or tenant small pieces of land. One estimate however indicates
that the proportion of landless has increased from 13% of rural
households in 1891 to 38% in 1931 (Moore 1966: 368). This increase does not mean that farm sizes for other peasants have
increased. Rather, it means that population increases have made
it impossible for many peasants to find a plot to cultivate. This
degree of economic differentiation of the peasant community has
not yet been reached in many other Asian countries such as Burma
and Thailand, and it was never reached to any serious extent in
Japan. But by the mid-twentieth century we find in rural India a
substantial landlord class letting out its land in small plots to
peasant households, and a rural proletariat with little or no land
either owned or tenanted.

Perhaps the most depressing aspect of Indian rural society at
present is the parasitic nature of the landlord class. This class seems

uninterested in investing its resources in agricultural improvements which might increase the return from these lands, or in using
its influence within the village community to promote community
development activities or agricultural innovation. Its main concern
is to get its rents on time and to ensure that its standing in the village is not jeopardized in any way. This is unfortunate since the
landlord class is probably in the best position to learn about innovations and to find the resources necessary to take advantage of
new farming opportunities. According to Myrdal's analysis, the
explanation for this passivity is to be derived from the structure of
the institutions described above. There is overwhelming evidence
that opportunities do exist for agricultural investments which
could raise India's grain yields and which would yield large returns in income, since prices for foodstuffs in India have increased
substantially in the last decade (Etienne 1968:83). There are striking differences of output in different districts within states and
within particular villages which cannot be explained simply in
terms of soil qualities and other natural factors. However, to utilize
these opportunities requires effort, a desire for increased income,
and some willingness to accept the problems attendant upon dis-
rupting the local community should he actually farm his land
directly (Heston 1968; Mellor 1966).

The landlord is not likely to accept this challenge for a number
of reasons. One of the most important of these derives from the
structure of the stratification system in rural India, which derives
in turn largely from the economic differentiation described above.
It is true that the values now associated with the various castes in
India can be traced back to the pre-British period, but there can
be little doubt that subsequent economic differentiation has served
to perpetuate and extend these values. Since agricultural labor is
associated with those positions in rural society receiving the least
power and wealth, labor itself tends to be negatively or invidiously
evaluated. To be able to avoid labor thus becomes an important
symbol of prestige in such a community, and an end to which its
members aspire (Myrdal 1968:1067; Fukutake 1964:142). It is likely
that the more differentiated a community becomes on any reward

dimension, the more important these rewards become to its members, since they have more to gain or lose. In these Indian communities, to be able to maintain a leisured life style is thus of great significance to the local landed elite, as is the ability to affect a level of consumption which clearly differentiates the elite from those at lower levels of the status system. Extraordinary tensions can be aroused in Indian rural communities when any group within it does not conform to prevailing standards set by caste rules (Lewis 1958:55-86).

Given this background, we should not be surprised at the landlord's reluctance to involve himself in farming activities, and his tendency to move out of the village altogether, nor at the peasant's desire to quit farming whenever he attains an income making this possible. Despite this, we might still expect some pressure on the landlord to increase his income. Even where traditional consumption standards have been uninfluenced by wider access to urban products, it would be a rare landlord who could not use some increase in income, if only to better manage his traditional obligations (Wiser and Wiser 1960:202). But even this pressure has been muted by the fact that the landlord can often increase his income simply by sitting back and letting prospective tenants bid up the price of his rentals. Price increases for food grains have also facilitated this process. The landlord may also prefer to use any surplus capital he has in the lucrative business of moneylending—there being no lack of claimants for loans in the contemporary Indian village.

The landlord class would seem capable of vigorous action only if it becomes infused with new members from urban areas where committment to the ideal of profit maximization could perhaps overcome the scruples about labor held by the old rural landowning class. Urban influences can also substantially raise the consumption standards now prevalent in the rural community. Such infusions have been important elsewhere, including England, and even in some parts of India. Thus in certain areas of Madras, landlords from the urban areas have been instrumental in expanding rice yields (Moore 1966:399-400). However, given the Indian government's reluctance to permit further accumulation of land in the hands of landlords, it is unlikely that this pattern will occur on a large scale.

The effects of Indian land-tenure institutions on the other major strata are equally disturbing. The sharecropping arrangement under which the tenant labors, and the insecurity of his tenure remove much of his incentive to invest (Myrdal 1968:1064-1066). Any long-term improvements he makes to his land are likely to lead to subsequent increases in his rents. In any case, the level of his rental usually leaves him with very little beyond minimum subsistence needs. The owner-occupier is in a much stronger financial position to take advantage of new opportunities, and the evidence does indeed indicate that he has been the most active innovator in rural India (Myrdal 1968:1068). Yet the tiny size of his holding does not leave him much margin for investment, and with continuing population pressures and increased exposure to market pressures, his holdings are likely to diminish in size. If experience elsewhere in Asia is a valid guide, and if the government does not interfere, the level of tenancy in those areas most subject to commercialization is likely to increase.

The small owner-occupiers and the tenant farmers are still essentially subsistence farmers; it is difficult to see how they would change this orientation given the constant pressure on them just to maintain their positions in society. They do not perceive agriculture as a business venture oriented towards profit, but rather as a way of life or, more bleakly, as a means of survival (Bose 1962:557). They do not have connections outside the village or the time to learn about agricultural innovations, nor can they afford the risks frequently associated with innovations disseminated by the Indian Community Development Program. Near the bottom of the stratification system, with little hope of raising their status, there is little to encourage them to believe that progress in the system is possible. As for the expanding class of landless laborers, the hopelessness of their situation is distressingly evident. In addition to the economic and political deprivations they suffer through not possessing land, they also suffer the indignities of their low position in the caste system (often as untouchables). It is not surprising that we find what might be referred to as a "culture of poverty" amongst the tenants and laborers. Among other characteristics, this involves a sense of hopelessness or disinterest in the future which is difficult to break through even when genuine opportunities are offered. (Cf. Etienne 1968:98.)

The reluctance of the Indian federal and state governments to legislate more aggressive programs for enforcing agricultural investment and innovation can itself be understood partly in terms of the land-tenure system. Thus any effort to seriously increase taxation (which at present is very low for farmers) or to enforce increased investment or innovations on landlords, would be resisted by the landlord class, and since they have considerable political influence within the village—where most of the electorate resides— it would be political suicide for the incumbent governments to legislate such action (cf. Hart 1967; Bailey 1957; Lewis 1964).

The situation we have in India, then, is that increases in population seem to have stimulated parallel increases in production as peasants have cultivated their smaller plots more intensively or have expanded their holdings into marginal lands in order to survive (Heston 1968:175). This pattern seems to have been typical in agrarian history; it is only in the last few centuries that agricultural productivity in a few societies has expanded much beyond that needed for subsistence by a growing population (Geertz 1963:77-8; Boserup 1965).

The English Experience

In discussing the English case my goal is to see whether land tenure and related social institutions in rural England were different from those of India; if so whether these differences have been significant in determining the relatively successful modernization of English agriculture. I will try to identify the major factors which shaped these differences in land-tenure institutions.

It is difficult to draw any firm conclusions from a comparison of two societies as different as England and India. Yet at a very general level there do seem to be a number of parallels in the structure of rural society in the two countries prior to the onset of agricultural modernization, as well as some significant parallels in the forces of population increase, commercialization and political change. Thus it is at least plausible to ascribe some causal weight to those differences in their historical background and to the forces which appear relevant to agricultural development as determinants of the sharply dissimilar outcome as to agricultural productivity and the structure of rural institutions in contemporary India and nineteenth century England. For example, in nineteenth century England, an even higher proportion of land was in the hands of landlords than in contemporary India. But in contrast to India, the English landlord often invested large amounts of capital in his property and, what may be even more important, let out large parcels of a hundred acres or more to capitalistic farmers, although as in India, there was no lack of peasants vying for tenancies of much smaller size.

During the nineteenth century these English farmers, in sharp contrast to the contemporary Indian peasant, proved themselves highly responsive to the opportunities provided by the availability of new inputs (agricultural machinery, chemical fertilizer, etc.). At least until 1850, England agriculture was able to supply most of the agricultural needs of the rapidly expanding urban population. But why and to what extent did the social institutions we have discussed influence these developments? The problem is exceedingly complex, and certainly no single factor provides an adequate explanation for these events. But the key to this puzzle may lie in the differing social background and subsequently divergent political, economic and other pressures faced by the landlord in the two societies.

Prior to the sixteenth century in England, land was generally held by the lord of the manor, and cultivated for him by tenants who were to various degrees tied to the land. The tenants were usually subject to services beyond the simple payment of rent in kind; however, they held hereditary rights to the land they cultivated and to the commons and wastes of the village. These rights could not easily be abrogated by the lord, nor could their rental obligations be easily altered. The lord was primarily concerned with meeting his consumption, service and military needs from his estate, rather than with making a profit.

This situation changed during the sixteenth and subsequent centuries with increases in demand for agricultural products (especially wool) from the expanding urban areas within England and elsewhere in Europe. The land and its products became valuable economic investments which the old landowning class and a new landlord class from the urban areas began to recognize (Chambers and Mingay 1966:19). Though it is hard to assess the extent of land purchases by this latter class, its predominance was far greater than in contemporary India. The English urban rich sought to own and live on a rural estate since they were anxious to turn their wealth into the style of life of the landed gentry. But these men brought with them a capitalistic orientation to the land; they were freer from the influences of the traditional rural community and its way of life than the old landowning class, and less willing to submit to the pressures from the peasants to maintain the old system (cf. Hoskins 1957:199).

This process was not one whereby a new landlord class simply replaced the old or where peasant households continued to work their small plots for different landlords. In fact many of the old landowning class did retain possession of rural estates, some expanding them substantially. The old elite was not beyond taking action opposed to the interests of the peasants, for many of the Tudor enclosures of arable land for pastoral farms were carried out by this class, causing considerable disruption to the peasants' lives. These estate owners, however, often had intricate social, political, and business connections with the urban world and were far less isolated from urban influences than the old landowning class of rural India. Also, some landlords and large farmers emerged from within the village community itself, viz. the development of the famed English yeoman. What is most interesting from the standpoint of the comparative analysis is that we find in England between the sixteenth and nineteenth centuries a process within the village of economic and social differentiation in some ways similar to what happened in India during the nineteenth and twentieth centuries. Peasants who owned or held rights to tenant land lost this land to the landlord class, whatever its background. In the dissolution of the manorial system during this period, many peasants lost control over their land. Many tenants who had been tied to the land under the manorial system lost their traditional tenancy rights with fixed rents. Some became tenant farmers unprotected by traditional rights; others became landless laborers.

This process of economic differentiation had gone a long way even before the Parliamentary Enclosure movement of the eighteenth century. By the beginning of the eighteenth century there were more landless laborers in England than owner-occupiers or tenant farmers. These developments can be ascribed to the same pressures we found operating in India; that is, population growth, commercialization of agriculture and political changes. Population growth forced the fragmentation of holdings, while commercialization increased the peasants' needs for cash just when he was becoming increasingly vulnerable to crisis. These pressures enabled the landlord to take advantage of the peasant, usually through the process of peasant indebtedness, which ultimately tended to force the peasant to sell his land to meet the debt.

The Parliamentary Enclosures of the eighteenth and early nineteenth centuries accentuated this process of economic differentiation in the following way. Ideally, all members of the village were to receive allotments in the enclosure settlements; however, many cottagers and squatters who had eked out a living on tiny farms augmented by their use of the commons and wastes did not receive allotments (Tate 1967:174). Those small holders who did receive allotments often found that the costs of enclosure and subsequent capital costs of fencing and ditching, plus the loss of their common rights, made it impossible for them to survive as owner-occupiers. The Enclosure Acts were particularly effective in destroying what remained of the peasants' rights to the commons and to the land they cultivated or tenanted which remained from the old manorial system (Martin 1967:138-9; Hoskins 1957:264).

The English landlord's involvement in the improvement of his property and his practice of letting it out in large consolidated farms seems to have been of great significance in the successful modernization of English agriculture. It also indicates that not all forms of inequitable land distribution constitute blockages to agricultural progress. The question we must now ask is why the English landlord did not follow the practice (as in India) of letting his land out in small plots to individual peasant households, leaving the improvement of its earning capacity to his tenants? This should help us understand why the equally inequitable distribution of land in India has turned out to be a depressant rather than a stimulant to agricultural development.

It should be noted that there was considerable resistance from the smaller peasants against this development. The English peasant owner-occupier fought bitterly to avoid losing his land, as did the tenant to avoid losing his tenancy. He was threatened by loss of the prestige of farming his own lot as well as much of his economic security since he was now dependent on other farmers for work. The peasants were also opposed to the break up of the open field system of cultivation: an unfenced three-field system in which farmers cultivated scattered strips in each field according to a rotation decided on by the community. The poorer peasants were especially reluctant to give up their rights to the commons and wastes which the village community had also controlled (Chambers and Mingay 1966:86). Thus we find evidence of cottagers holding just an acre or two plus the right to graze a few animals in the commons preferring to continue with this marginal livelihood rather than work as agricultural laborers (Hammond and Hammond 1927:13-14). It was no simple matter for the landlord to consolidate his lands and tenant them as large farms. It required considerable desire and much financial and political power to overcome the moral outrage and political opposition of most of the village community.

In eighteenth and nineteenth century England, it was difficult, though not impossible, to take advantage of the agricultural innovations abroad at the time without the use of large consolidated plots (Havinden 1967:66-79). Even changes in farming practices not requiring land consolidation were difficult to effect since in the open field system (which prevailed over more than half of England at the beginning of the eighteenth century), permission to deviate from established agricultural practices usually had to be gained from the community as a whole, and this was often a difficult and cumbersome process (Hammond and Hammond 1927: 13-14; Hoskins 1957:238-240). The major innovations available were the use of sown grasses (especially clover) and root crops (turnips, swedes, etc.) in rotation with wheat or some other cereal (Chambers and Mingay 1966:54-56). These innovations simultaneously enriched the soil and provided more fodder for the farmer's cattle. This enabled the farmer to increase the number of his cattle, which in turn increased the supply of manure, which when carefully collected and applied further enriched the soil. It was difficult to incorporate these innovations into the open field system since the old rotation system including the fallow had to be abolished. The pattern of grazing cattle communally on the commons and in the fallow were also hindrances to the new practices since the farmer with cattle was anxious to graze or fold them in his own fields in order not to lose any of the dung.

By enclosing his land the landlord could gain considerable increases in rent; perhaps double the pre-enclosure rent. It was also in his interest to have the commons and wastes enclosed, for he was alloted a share of this land from which he previously might have received no income and which would be greatly improved by careful cultivation (Chambers and Mingay 1966:79-83). Those cottagers and squatters who had previously eked out a living on the commons and wastes were now generally forced to become agricultural laborers, a circumstance favorable to the large farmer since it increased the supply of labor (Hammond and Hammond 1927: 13-14). Finally, enclosure through Act of Parliament wiped out any residues of traditional rights tenants could claim from their lords, including any vestiges of rental levels fixed by tradition (Tate 1967:155).

It is fairly easy to understand why the landlord was in favor of enclosure, but it is not quite so clear why he tended increasingly in the eighteenth and nineteenth century to lease his land to larger farmers. The answer to this question would seem to lie in the extent and nature of the investments necessary and economies of scale involved in taking advantage of the innovations described above. Either the landlord or the tenant had to invest considerable cash in increasing the number of his livestock, in hedging or fencing, in buildings (especially cattle pens or barns) and sometimes in marling or draining the land. The small holder had more difficulty contributing this capital, and since there were also some economies of scale, the small farmer (unlike his Indian counterpart) could less effectively compete with the large farmer. The crucial difference is that many of the innovations involved in intensive Asian farming require investments of labor rather than cash; here the small farmer can compete better, since he can usually invest his own and his family's labor at rates lower than those hired laborers would have to be paid. Finally, the landlord was probably anxious to put his expensive investment (his land) in the hands of wealthy tenants who were less committed to the old peasant farming traditions and who were likely to make the best use of it. In the post-enclosure period, no landowner had trouble finding cheap labor to help in cultivation.

The small peasants, then, were opposed to the enclosure of the open fields and to the expansion of the size of farms. There is no question that enclosure and increased farm size would have been delayed or not taken place at all had it not been for the political strength of the landlord class. In fact, in few other areas in Europe do we find developments similar to the English case. In most European countries, farm sizes, even by the mid 1930's, remained well under half the average size of the British farm (Warriner 1964: 3; cf. Grigg 1966:89). One exception to this is Prussia, where the commercial demands for food, and the political power of the landlords seem to have led to enclosure and consolidation practices similar to England (Landes 1962:103). Despite the English landlord's political influence in the eighteenth and early nineteenth centuries, he was fortunate to avoid a number of political reper-

cussions which might have undermined his freedom to act as he
did. Perhaps the landlord was only saved by the Speenhamland
system of public relief, and later in the nineteenth century, when
the peasant received the vote, by the employment opportunities
offered by British industry and commerce.

One final point we should discuss, given the sharp differences
between the English and Indian experience, is the importance of
industrialization in shaping the activities of landlords and farmers.
In the latter part of the period we are considering (late eighteenth
century), English industrialization was well under way, but no
equivalent development has yet occurred in India. I think this
factor is important though the influences of industrialization are so
extensive as to be difficult to specify.

It should first be noted that industrialization had little to do
with the agricultural innovations that we argued were so important in prompting the landlord's actions. It was only in the
second half of the nineteenth century that new industries made
much direct contribution to agricultural technology, since it was
only then that agricultural machinery, chemical fertilizers, etc.
were made available on a large scale (Chambers and Mingay
1966:2). (Incidentally, if chemical fertilizers had been available in
the eighteenth century in large and cheap quantities there probably would have been much less pressure for changed tenure arrangements in England, since fertility could have been improved
without the clovers, roots and cattle dung.)

We can note a variety of ways that industrialization did influence the behavior of landlords and farmers. First, it helped in
crease the demand for agricultural products, which meant substantially increased prices—especially during the Napoleonic wars
—thereby making agriculture a more profitable investment. But
this factor, though important, by itself cannot account for English
developments, since similar movements in prices in India during
and since World War II have not produced parallel consequences.
Second, the expansion of the mercantile and industrial monied
class does seem to have been important in providing a source for
enterprising capitalist leadership in agriculture, something that

India has not experienced as yet. Finally, commercial and industrial development helped expand the supply of capital that rural
investors could draw on. The availability of capital at very low
rates of 4-5% by the eighteenth century helped the English landowner and his tenants handle the costs of enclosure and the investments necessary to take advantage of the more advanced agricultural technology available at the time. Agriculture also benefited
from investments in transport and communications stimulated
by industrialization. However here one must be careful in general-
izing, for this capital flow was a two-way process: agriculture provided much of England's tax income at this time (Chambers and
Mingay 1966:44; Deane 1965:49-50).

By the early nineteenth century the process of economic differentiation in the English village had concentrated land in the hands
of a wealthy and commercially oriented landlord class which was
most likely to exploit its productive potential. In their concern to
do this, the English landlords were instrumental in sweeping away
most of the remaining traditional restrictions on the rational use
of land. Finally, the landlords let out their land to substantial
tenants in large farms, and often assisted these tenants in improving the quality of the land and its equipment. These developments
appear to have facilitated the response of English farmers to the
demands for food in the nineteenth century. Thus between 1750
and 1850 the average wheat yield in England nearly doubled and
English farmers were able to supply most of the food requirements
of a population which expanded from 8.9 million in 1781 to 20.8
million in 1851. Finally when industry began to produce new agricultural machines, chemical fertilizers, etc. in the second half of
the nineteenth century the farmer was able to respond relatively
effectively to these opportunities (Grigg 1966:2; Deane and Cole
1962:8).

Obviously the concentration of land in the hands of landlords
is not in itself a factor sufficient to determine agricultural development. In India the landlord-tenant relationship seems to have been
an obstacle to agricultural progress, whereas in England it was a
major stimulant. The landlord is not inevitably a social parasite

or an enterpreneur. To understand his behavior we have to know a great deal about his social background and the social, economic and political pressures he is subject to in dealing with his land. The same is true of the farmer, whether large or small.

I think the analysis has highlighted the significance of several factors capable of influencing the behavior of landlords and farmers in the two societies thus far examined. The first is the importance of the social background of the landlord, especially whether he is recruited from an old landowning class or from a class with different experiences and values. Second is the ecological structure of agriculture and its relation to the economic requirements for improving the productivity of the land. (It goes without saying that purely economic factors such as food prices, the costs of capital, labor costs, etc., are also important determinants.) Finally, the analysis points to the importance of the political strength of the various groups with interests in change or continuity of traditional peasant patterns of behavior.

THE JAPANESE EXPERIENCE

In the light of the preceding discussion, the Japanese experience is of particular interest, for the Japanese managed to develop their rural economy between 1868 and 1914 far beyond the point attained by most South Asian societies even today, yet they did so on the basis of an institutional structure in many ways similar to that of contemporary India. In one sense, the Japanese experience between 1868 and 1914 is more difficult to explain than the English case since there are fewer differences between Japanese and Indian tenure institutions than between those of India and England. Yet we have evidence that between 1868 and 1914 agricultural production in Japan increased at an annual rate of 2% or more, while agricultural population actually fell slightly during the same time (FAO 1967:479; cf. Rosovsky 1968). This of course is a striking performance as compared with Indian agriculture in the last twenty years, especially when the point of comparison is labor productivity.

What were the major similarities between Indian and Japanese land tenure institutions? During the Tokugawa period there had been considerable growth in the Japanese rural population, and an increase in the commercialization of agriculture. With these developments came the familiar process of economic differentiation within the peasant community. By the 1880's the amount of land tenanted in Japan was as great or greater than we find in contemporary India (Smith 1959:163). Also as in India, the land was let out in small holdings to peasant households, there being little or no consolidation of farms at this time. Japanese tenancy arrangements were also similar to the Indian in that the tenant had little security of tenure and no means of gaining compensation for land improvements he might make (Kawano 1965:141). The apparent similarities between Japan and India emphasize the point made at the conclusion of the section on England: a knowledge of land distribution and the mechanics of the tenancy system do not take us far in explaining agricultural progress. In the following analysis, therefore, I will attempt to delineate the different pressures influencing the behavior of landlords and farmers in India and Japan.

To follow the pattern set in the previous discussion we might first ask whether the social background of the Japanese landlord was of importance. It probably was, for the Japanese landlord emerged from within the village itself rather than being recruited from the ranks of the military aristocracy (the Samurai), whose values were explicitly anti-mercantile. Very few Samurai turned to farming in the Meiji period (1868-1912). The landlord class in Japan had, however, been intimately involved in business and farming during the Tokugawa period, and though there were some breakdowns in the patterns of exclusion, no upward mobility to the status of the Samurai had been permitted (Moore 1966:275; Smith 1959). There is thus an interesting contrast with the Indian case, in that the Indian landlord is frequently a Brahmin who tends to uphold anti-mercantile values derived from his aristocratic and priestly background.

When we turn to an analysis of the various social economic and political pressures the landlord and peasant farmer were subject to during the Meiji period, it appears that most of the differences between the Indian and Japanese situation derive from differences in the rates of industrialization in the two societies. The ecology and farm technology of Indian and Japanese agriculture are certainly much closer to one another than either is to English agriculture. Nor did the political power of the Japanese landlord in the Meiji period differ much from that of the landlord in contemporary India.

How then did the differential rate of industrialization influence agricultural development? There has already been some discussion of this question in the literature. Clifford Geertz and Barrington Moore, Jr., emphasize the effects which investment of the rural surplus in industrial capital has subsequently had on agricultural growth. Geertz (1963) argues that these effects derive primarily from the ability of Japanese industry to provide cheap new inputs, notably chemical fertilizer to farmers, and secondarily from the absorption of the surplus rural population in urban employment. Moore (1966:344) sees a similar process in India though he places greater emphasis on the role of the parasitic landlord and moneylender in squandering the rural surplus than on the outflow of capital to Britain. However, it was not until after World War I that Japanese farmers began to use chemical fertilizer, and not until the 1920's did Japanese industry begin to produce chemical fertilizers in volume (Nobufume 1964:382). The major technical innovations responsible for production increases up to 1914 were the extension of the irrigation system, increases in fertilizer inputs (including soya bean cake and night soil), improved seed, and more intensive cultivation techniques. These factors did not directly depend on the growth of Japanese industry.

The effects of industrialization on rural population growth seem to be of more significance. Increases in Japanese rural population (which were, in any case, much lower than contemporary India) were largely absorbed in the urban areas and to some extent in rural industry. This had several consequences, most of which derived from the diminished pressure on the already tiny farms.

First, rural Japan never developed a class of landless laborers of the proportion we now find in India. In fact, in late Tokugawa times there were continuing complaints about shortages of rural labor (Smith 1959:120). Thus the Japanese never suffered the same wastage of labor we find in India today (Myrdal 1968:1088-9). Neither do we find the same negative evaluation of manual labor in rural Japan as in India (Beardsley et al. 1959:68). This may be partly because in the absence of a lower class that must hire its labor to others invidious distinctions against labor are less likely to develop in the village community.

Second, Japanese farmers were not pushed any closer to subsistence by these developments; rather, as prices and production increased and as taxes declined, the standard of living of the average peasant must have improved. This made it easier for him to find capital to invest in his farm, and lessened the tendencies to indebtedness such as we find among poor Indian peasants. It also weakened the position of the landlord as compared with his Indian counterpart, since we do not find either competition for land or increases in tenancy rates. Nor do we find any increase in the amount of land tenanted between the late nineteenth century and World War II. It may have been the weaker bargaining position of the Japanese landlord combined with his lack of prejudice against commercial activities that made him active in investing in his property and in encouraging his tenants to do likewise (Dore 1959:47). It would seem plausible that if he wanted increases in his income he would have to be more active than the Indian landlord in such investment, but I must admit that this is largely speculation on my part.

Several other characteristics of Japanese rural society differ from India and seem to be important. The Japanese rural community was much less stratified and factionalized than the Indian village; as a result, the landlord who did respond to the government's exhortations that he promote innovations such as improved seed, was willing to do so since any disruptions in the village stratification system were of less significance to him than to his Indian counterpart (Dore 1965:492). With the break up of feudal restrictions on the mobility of capital, labor, information, and other resources, innovations from the more highly developed areas of Japan spread relatively quickly to the more backward areas, rapidly boosting production in these areas (Rosovsky 1968:358). Indeed, if Smith's analysis of the extent of commercial forces in rural Japan by the end of the Tokugawa period is correct, we would certainly expect a rapid response from these peasants to the opportunities created by the Meiji reforms (Smith 1959).

It is difficult for me to estimate the significance of each of these factors, as detailed information in English on the structure of the Meiji agriculture is limited. However, as a group they do give some explanation of why Japanese agriculture managed as well as it did during the period. Yet as compared with English agriculture it would seem that Japanese agriculture improved in the Meiji period in spite of its land tenure institutions rather than because of them. After World War I, agricultural growth diminished in Japan, and the landlord, who seems to have become increasingly parasitic, came to be perceived as a social and economic problem.

As we have seen, the pathways to agricultural modernization in England and Japan have been sharply divergent. Whereas English rural institutions by the nineteenth century seem to have facilitated technical innovations and made possible substantial increases in farm incomes, the same is less true for Japan. The tiny farm has continued as the basis of Japanese agriculture since 1946. Though significant increases in per acre productivity have been attained, especially in the last decade, Japanese agriculture is now considered a problem industry by the standards of the rest of Japanese society

Myrdall (1968:1370-1375) believes that land reform is the most important institutional reform that the Indian government could make at present, and he argues that other programs are not likely to have much effect without it. The Japanese land reform program since World War II comes very close to the form Myrdal proposes for India, since it created a remarkably equitable distribution of land, and subsequent legislation has protected the farmer from pressures to alienate his land. But has this reform stimulated progress in rural Japan? And to what extent is the Japanese reform relevant to rural problems in India?

Agricultural production since the reform has increased substantially, averaging 4% yearly between 1955 and 1965 despite some decline in the number of farmers (Fukutake 1967:59). It seems that some of this growth was facilitated by the land reform. Pride of ownership, security of tenure, and increases in income, especially amongst former tenants, all seem to have increased the confidence of the peasant and helped to make him more responsive to innovation (Ouchi 1966:140). However these developments have occurred under conditions not at all comparable with those existing in India today. For the Japanese farmer is now inextricably enmeshed in a highly industrialized, mass consumption society, and it is unlikely that he would have attained the production levels of the 1960's without this involvement. This society has made it possible for most farmers to become literate, and has exposed them to a barrage of communications about modern consumption styles. According to Fukutake (1967:55), 70% of Japanese farm households now have T.V. This has prevented the small farmer from simply consuming the produce of his farm. The contemporary Japanese farmer's anxiety to attain middle class consumption standards—complete with visits to the beauty parlor for his wife— has been a crucial stimulant to investment. Without investment he could not attain the increases in income desired to make these standards a reality. Also, Japanese industry now provides at low cost the chemical fertilizer and the agricultural machinery so important for increases in labor productivity. Moreover the Japanese government now subsidizes the price of agricultural commodities to ensure at least the maintenance of the farmer's income. Thus it would be dangerous to assume that land reform by itself could accomplish the same results in India as in contemporary Japan. Myrdal has not argued from the Japanese experience; however the warning is still appropriate, for it is tempting to use this experience as justification for land reform policies elsewhere in Asia.

Agriculture is now considered a problem industry in Japan be-

cause, although farmers incomes have increased, they have not
kept pace with those of most urban workers. In response to this
situation there has recently been a substantial out-migration,
mainly of younger men to the urban areas—so much so that between 1960 and 1965 rural population fell from 13.7 to 11.5
million, (a figure below the 1939 level) (Fukutake 1967:59). The
source of the problem partly lies in the equality of land distribution and the legislation limiting land alienation, for it is extremely
difficult for a farm household with a couple of acres to make an
income comparable with that of an urban worker. The recent
gains in production have come mainly from more intensive cultivation (meaning more labor input), the addition of more chemical
fertilizer, and the development of seeds capable of responding to
these inputs. It may be that diminishing returns are beginning to
occur both for labor and capital from these practices; for example,
one expert suggests that the ability of the rice plant to absorb
further chemicals has been dropping in recent years. (Nobufume
1964:390). In any case, substantially higher returns per farmer
must now come from increased labor productivity; but this is only
likely to occur if the acreage of farms is increased. Should this
occur the farmer could take maximum advantage of the agricultural machinery designed for Japanese rice growing conditions.
Since 1961, it has become declared government policy to promote
farm consolidation. In other words, though land reform which per-
petuates the tiny farm may under certain conditions contribute to
production increases, in the long run it may not be a satisfactory
institutional basis for agricultural development.

CONCLUSION

According to Myrdal's theory as developed with reference to
India, traditional land tenure institutions, notably inequality
of land ownership and the fragmentation of farm size, have been
significant obstacles to agricultural progress. This is because the
ecological structure of rice production in India and the competition among peasants for scarce land have favored the emergence

of the parasitic landlord. This behavior has been reinforced by developments in related institutions, especially the rural stratification system, and in the value systems of the various strata making it up.

Our analysis of the English and Japanese cases has, I think, confirmed the importance of land tenure institutions in determining agricultural progress. However, I have argued that for an adequate theory of agricultural development one must go beyond the structure of the land tenure institutions to the factors which shape the behavior of the landlords and tenants. The English case indicates that landlords can behave in both favorable and unfavorable ways *vis à vis* agricultural development. Similarly it was argued that while equality of land distribution has been an effective reform in contemporary Japan, it may not work in a more backward or less industrialized society.

The analysis has also highlighted some of the major conditions which have influenced the Indian land tenure system to work so unfavorably for agricultural development. The major factors isolated were as follows: First, the social background of the landlord, and the extent he is tied to a commercial rather than an aristocratic or traditional rural culture. Second, the ecological structure of Asian rice culture and the extent to which it has favored the competitive position of the smaller peasant. Third, the pressures of population growth and industrialization which have affected the power of the landlord in relation to the price he can charge for the right to tenant his land. Fourth, the profits that acceptance of innovations can bring to the landlord or farmer. Finally, the political power of the landlord, as it has enabled him to protect his vested interests in the old system, or supported him as he sought to innovate at the expense of the smaller peasants. Any predictions about the consequences of tenure reforms would, at the very least, have to take account of each of these factors.

The anaysis of Japanese materials casts some suspicion on land reform as a solution to India's problems, for it indicates that inequality of land ownership is not the major problem but rather the conditions indicated above which make the landlord and farmer behave as they do. Their behavior would probably change if these conditions changed. The real hope for Indian agriculture would appear to lie in rapid industrialization or, alternatively, in developments which would increase the competitive power of the tenant, or increase the landlord's need for income enough that he would have to invest in his property to gain this income. I am not the first to hope that the political power, wealth, prestige and supra-village connections of the Indian landlord might be turned to the advantage of Indian agriculture. Thus the British hoped, forlornly as it turned out, that the nineteenth century Zamindar would emulate the enterprising English landlord we discussed above. No doubt it would take a dramatic change in the pressures impinging on the Indian landlord to diminish his parasitic inclinations, considering the factors which now tend to reinforce such behavior. However, land reform in contemporary India might simply consilidate the small peasant subsistence system which is not necessarily a favorable institutional system for agricultural progress.

DAVID BURLESON

As Healthy as a Peasant

So we have a population explosion. It is real. It is dire. It is accelerating. It is mixed with religion, involved in politics. It is hope of the business-man where there is too much, and the bane of progress where there is too little. It causes war, pestilence, and famine. It is an ogre that rides all four horses of the Apocalypse and spurs them on. Why did it have to wait until we are at our wits' end with other problems to spring at us now? (Garst 1963:3).

If the fact of more living human beings were to be taken as a measure of health, then the world could be considered healthier than it has ever been. Demographic estimates indicate that the world population was only about 250 million at the time of Christ; by A.D. 1650, it was about 500 million. In 1960, world population was estimated to be 3 billion, and by the end of the twentieth century it is expected to reach a number in excess of 6 billion. The miracles of modern medicine have eliminated or controlled a number of infectious diseases as major causes of death. Since the end of the Second World War, growth rates of world population have doubled from 1 per cent per annum to 2 per cent. Life expectancy rates have gone up almost everywhere. Even in a nation with all the economic, social and health problems which India has, life expectancy jumped from 27 years to 42 years in the first eleven years of independence. The poor nations are experiencing a population growth unprecedented in human history. This population explosion places greater demands upon agricultural and industrial resources at the same time that increased demands are made in the revolution of rising expectations.

For one-third of the present world population this planet is a reasonably healthy place, but for the other two-thirds our world is not nearly such a hospitable ecosphere. When Thoreau concluded that "Most men live lives of quiet desperation," he was not thinking particularly of public health problems. Now, however, it seems thoroughly reasonable to conclude that in this last third of the twentieth century most men live lives as healthy and quietly desperate as a peasant. Many wonder where the next meal is going to come from. This is despair, yet the term *desperation* does not necessarily ring true within the framework of traditional cultures. In looking at the peasant and his culture in his own terms, we often find something quite different from despair. We find methods of coping. Very frequently we find fatalism.

Erasmus analyzes the concept of fatalism as a major component in a traditional society. As he describes the case:

Much of the peasant's seeming apathy and unconcern results from the prevalent attitudes that it does not really matter what is done to help a person if his time has come to die. Life, in a sense, is cheaper among many of the underprivileged peoples of the world because they have a much higher expectation of death than we do. If no one is to be blamed or made the scapegoat for illness and death, as is the case in areas where witchcraft is greatly feared, fatalism will probably be common. (Erasmus 1961:52)

In spite of economic progress in many nations, societies continue to be extremely heterogeneous and health to be disproportionately shared. Mexico is a well-documented case in point. Casanova presents the plus-and-minus aspects of Mexican development:

Differences exist not only between those who have little and those who have much, but also between those who have something and those who have nothing at all. The rural population makes up 49 per cent of the total and without doubt is the poorest; 38 per cent of the people are still illiterate; 37 per cent of the children of school age are not in school; 38 per cent of the people still go barefoot; 24 percent eat no meat, no fish, no eggs, and never drink milk. The number of Mexicans who live on a bare-subsistence level today is at least equal to the number in the past. The rate of development has been insufficient to counteract numerically the high rate of increase of the population as a whole (Casanova 1964).

In other words, the have and have-not situation in Mexico, a country with an enormous peasantry, is not unlike the international situation documented in economic literature on the rich and poor nations. The United States, with 6 per cent of the world population, consumes 60 per cent of each year's industrial resource production, and yet one-fifth of the populace is considered to below the "poverty line."

One more macroscopic observation is necessary before turning to the peasantry. On March 13, 1961, when John Fitzgerald Kennedy proposed the Alliance for Progress, he said:

Throughout Latin America—a continent rich in resources and in the spiritual and cultural achievements of its people—millions of men and women suffer the daily degradations of hunger and poverty. They lack decent shelter or protection from disease. Their children are deprived of the education or the jobs which are the gateway to a better life. And each day the problems grow more urgent. Population growth is outpacing economic growth.

"As healthy as a peasant. . . ." What are we dealing with? In any society, even the most primitive, we have a number of factors working together (or not working together) to provide the members of that society with a way of life. Redfield describes culture as the total equipment of ideas and conventionalized activities (Redfield 1953:85). Concepts of health and illness are one important set of these ideas, helped or constrained by other sets. The preceding quotations indicate that rapid population growth, illiteracy, malnutrition, inadequate housing, war, and subsistence economics deal out a tough lot of cultural constraints for the peasants. The situation is practically one in which the peasants have to play against a stacked deck, with no trumps! Losses, such as the death of children in rural Mexico, are explained away as the creation of little angels.

I am taking a roundabout way to get at the core of the problem, "as healthy as a peasant." I am doing this for two reasons. First, I do not see any point in compiling yet another analysis of folk medicine. Polgar has given us an excellent analysis of health and human behavior and he provides an enormous bibliography on the social and cultural factors of health for the student who wants to study worldwide medical practices without donning a white coat (Polgar 1962). Caudill did a similar analysis a decade earlier (Caudill 1953). Second, I believe that too much of the literature in the anthropology and sociology of medicine is oriented toward ethnography rather than social anthropology, i.e., it is very descriptive of content rather than process. In the initial enthusiasm with which anthropology joined medicine and medicine became anthropologically fascinated during the past twenty years, the two disciplines have had great difficulty in being totally significant one to the other. The physicians have been asking patients: What's wrong with you? What have you done for your illness? Why haven't you. . . . ? What can we do for you? On the other hand, the anthropologists have been asking their informants: How do you cure *susto* (fright)? What do you do for *mal ojo* (evil eye)? Who made you sick? When you are sick, what do you do? For the most part, these questions are related to curative medicine.

The title of this paper pushes us to preventive medicine and the socio-cultural processes of healthiness: why are people as healthy as they are, and by what means are they so? For these questions and concerns we need to know far more epidemiology and ecology than either professional group has heretofore employed. We need to know the morbidity rates of peasants and we do not know them. Worse yet, we cannot accept the morbidity rates of rural hospitals as evidence because such statistics might not tell us anything more than who has the time to allow his or her illness to be registered. Adults may not have time to be sick! Before the modern miracle of DDT, millions upon millions of people in the world suffered malaria chronically or recurrently, so that a high degree of disease-specific morbidity was "normal" in the society. In Central America, surveys of rural school children indicate that it is not at all unusual for 90 per cent of the students to be suffering from intestinal worms. In the Chad, most of the adult population has, in the past, suffered onchocerciasis (river blindness) and a "normal" part of the socialization of children included having them serve as "seeing-eye guides" for their parents and other older relatives. Cases such as these dramatically indicate a cultural relativism about health and illness. Then Western medicine comes along, lowers the mortality rates, upsets the ecological relationships, and establishes the absolute goal of total health, defined by the World Health Organization as: "a state of complete physical, mental and social well-being."

It is obvious that modern medicine *and* hygiene have clearly demonstrated that prolonging life is really a rather easy thing to accomplish. Modern medicine has not yet devised similar or more imaginative means of accomplishing the state of complete physical, mental and social well-being. It is not, of course, entirely the task of health personnel to provide such methods. Society in one way or another has the task of making, defining and fulfilling itself. Given the nature of political organization in modern states and among states, this is going to require the elaboration of large regional patterns. Rats, lice and history have not been especially respectful of arbitrary political boundaries.

"As healthy as a peasant" hints that the peasant has some choice in matters of health in the modern world. It is probable that he does not. The peasant is about as efficient a producer as his technology permits (Moseman 1964), but his technology is no longer viable because his health has been improved—he lives longer—and his wife has the same number of pregnancies with more children surviving. The net result is that the size of the peasant family increases because infant mortality decreases rapidly and few peasants know about birth control, much less do anything about it. It is just too easy to drop the infant- and early-childhood mortality from 200 per thousand to 60, 70, or 80 per thousand without effecting any concomitant decrease in the birthrate. Thus, the peasant gets stuck with larger demands upon the same plot of land, be it his or his landlord's. The absolute food-consumption rates, mostly of calories, of most of the people in the Third World are dropping, a fact that leads us into a new situation of world crisis. This fact lends substance to prediction that the world is on the threshold of the biggest famine in history. Ewell contends that to provide the Third World with a minimum diet through 1980, grain production will have to double and the use of fertilizers will have to increase about ten times. (Ewell 1964). Ewell's world of the 1980's may prove more frightening than Orwell's. Garst, one of the three individuals most responsible for the diffusion of hybrid corn and nitrogen fertilizers in the United States, calculates that world famine could be averted over the next twenty years by an investment of approximately 20 billion dollars.

The rich nations are getting richer; the poor are having children and getting poorer. Nutritional levels in the poor nations are low, as they have been throughout history. Many of the worst nutritional problems, however, have been as attributable to ignorance and callousness as they have been to lack of nutrients as such. Thousands of children die of protein deficiency in areas where proteins which would save them do exist, and are often consumed in sufficient amounts in the *same* households where the children die for their lack. It is common practice among Central American peasants to give sick children only a grain gruel at the time when they most need proteins. Or, to push blame (a kind of rarified cultural-economic blame) to its extreme: eggs go to market, Coco-Cola is brought home. In 1964, 50 per cent of all deaths in El Salvador occurred in children under five years of age, and gastroenteric diseases were the major cause. Cleanliness—hygiene— and better dietary practices would have made an enormous difference in peasant and proletarian morbidity and mortality.

In Africa, as in Latin America, the greater part of the population is young; approximately 50 per cent of the total population is under fifteen years of age. Such an age structure in the population creates much dependency. Fewer people (adults) have to provide health, education, housing, etc., for the many minors. The opposite is the case in developed nations. When we think that some of the developing countries act in a juvenile manner we should consider that maybe they are just acting their age. Once a population or a segment of the population gets beyond the early years, the members are generally healthy. Thus, we see undeveloped nations achieve with relative ease mortality rates comparable to or even lower than the rates in developed nations. This is a temporary situation, however, and death rates will have to rise again. Meanwhile, healthy young adults are contributing greatly to the population explosion. The world population growth rate has doubled from 1 per cent at the end of the Second World War, and it will probably increase to 2.6 per cent per annum by 1980. Then the famine can start, and it will undoubtedly kill peasants and proletarians first.

The health problems of peasants in Africa make Latin America appear a paradise. Measles kills 15,000 children under fifteen years of age in Niger every year, even though vaccination costs less than one dollar per person. In 1967, the government of Kenya spent only a dollar and ten cents per capita for health. You do not buy much health (or curative or preventive medicine) with such limited quantities of cash. During the 1950's and early 1960's, in the Democratic Republic of the Congo, the prevalence rate for sleeping sickness fell to the very low figure of 0.1 per cent. In 1966, however, the rate was forty times greater and in some areas 14 per cent of the population had the disease. Under these circumstances, "as healthy as a peasant" does not mean much.

We have the same problem with the recurrence of malaria, or at least with the threat of recurrence. Despite all the health benefits and, in economic terms, even greater agricultural benefits which malaria control has produced in Central America, in 1964 the Pan American Health Organization had an uphill battle convincing El Salvador to keep up its work against malaria. In that year, El Salvador spent approximately 20 per cent of the national budget on health services, or about two dollars and eighty cents per person.

For the mountain dwellers of North Cameroon, the World Health Organization (with inadequate statistics, of course) has published the grave statement that life expectancy at birth is no more than twelve years. The Nutritional Institute of Central America and Panama is at present engaged in some very sophisticated research on nutrition and mental development, showing that babies start out all right and do well until weaning; then weanling diarrhea sets in and emerges as the major cause of death. Between the ages of eighteen months and three or four years the children receive inadequate protein and the developmental troubles, both physical and mental, begin. The culturally threatening conclusion which may well emerge from this research is that we may be forced to return to the use of the term "backward" for the peoples of the developing areas of the world. Increasing the life expectancy is one battle in the health field. Improving the mental and physical development within the longer life is no smaller battle.

"As healthy as a peasant" means a lot of things. Social change has accelerated in our century as in no other. Health, by international agreement, is coming to be thought of more and more as a right. "Good health" can be good economics: in 1942 there were at least two million cases of malaria in Greece; and ten years later there were less than 50,000. It was estimated that 40 million working days had been saved for the economy. Good health means that a great deal of informal or formal education has occurred. It means that, in Schweitzerian terms, there can be a greater respect for life, but also means that life can be further cheapened in some areas of the world because these areas and peoples are not prepared to cope with new demands of increased population upon their social organization and ecology. Modern medicine has major clues to relieving misery at the same time that better health (long-life, changed death rates without concomitant changes in birthrates, more life) provides another threat: overpopulaton.

For the past two decades those of us who read the population literature have been droned into believing that the rapid growth of population was second only in importance to the threat of nuclear warfare. Now the tone of the literature is changing and by the fact that nuclear war has been avoided for more than twenty years, *the experts* are moving the population problem into first place. (I think that the change is a correct one.) This problem allows Ewell to wax most eloquent and write:

It is hard for us sitting in rich, comfortable, overfed America to realize that the greatest disaster (famine) in the history of the world is just around the corner.

Historians of the future may remark whether it was more important to have devoted our resources during the 1960's to putting a man on the moon or to have devoted our resources toward averting the world famine of the 1970's. (Ewell, 1965: 109; 116).

Ewell puts the cost of averting this health crisis at five billion dollars as compared to Garst's figure of twenty billion. Either price makes us look like peasants compared to the fifty or so billion needed to see a man on the moon, or the seventy-plus billion we are obliging ourselves to spend on defense this year.

Typhus, cholera, plague, intestinal infestations, smallpox, malaria, poliomyelitis, syphilis, yaws, etc., are looked upon with dismay by modern man, yet they are very common in many parts of the world. It would be useless to cite additional statistics at this point; most of the statistics on disease for more than two out of three underdeveloped nations are inaccurate anyway. Yet several of these diseases are so common in some areas that they are regarded as nothing more than inconveniences and certainly not as great abnormalities.

Individual peasants and masses of peasants are going to continue to suffer these diseases and other illnesses, and if the dire, pessimistic predictions prove to be accurate, we will—according to

John Gordon, an emeritus professor of epidemiology at Harvard —see the mass recurrence of infectious diseases. The diseases will attack the weakened, malnourished constitutions first, but if they present themselves in particularly virulent forms they may well attack more than peasants and proletarians. The great influenza epidemic of the First World War and the relatively mild Asian Flu scare of 1957 are simpler cases of what might happen. Epidemics resemble great warnings that a disturbance has taken place in the development of a people.

Garst worries more about the hunger problem than about health. He believes that present agricultural technology is sufficient to feed the present world population but it will not necessarily be sufficient as we approach the millenium. He sees the role of the social scientist as changing from "grapher" to planner. In Redfieldian terms, the great tradition is going to have to provide much more know-how to the little tradition. The peasants have been good pragmatists in many aspects pertaining to their health, but they have become fatalistic when they have not had personal control. Modernization, aided by medical and paramedical personnel, will take away some of their control of their lives and give them more control of their physical health. All tendencies show that this is a price which traditional societies are willing to pay, even though the process is frequently a slow one (Caudill 1953; Polgar 1962).

I do not mean to end on a humorous note after having dealt with major sociopolitical problems of health and population, but I do believe, from four years of medical anthropology in one underdeveloped nation and a similar period of "population anthropology" in a variety of nations, that we need to ask "How are you?" as a basic question of social medicine. This question goes beyond the *what* and *when* questions I listed earlier and it has to be asked in health and in illness.

If we are to satisfy even a minimum of the World Health Organization's definition of health, we are going to have to learn a great deal more about human harmony than we presently know. Our value systems are going to have to change from first-order individualism and domination over nature to much stronger collateral relationships and collaboration with nature. The Navaho concept of harmony may present us with some clues. We will have to eliminate some of our practices which result in the rape of our natural environment and learn to appreciate the ecological value of wilderness areas, wetlands, and floods. The most affluent nation is history is quickly learning that material well-being does not guarantee happiness. Our psychosomatic illnesses indicate that something is very seriously wrong. It is trite to say that we have been guilty of placing material and mechanical values ahead of human values, but such seems very much to be the case. We spend millions on research for supersonic aircraft to add to the noise in our environment at the same time we have a poor people's march.

Peasants are not very healthy at the present time. In A.D. 2000 we are going to have a world population of between six and seven billion people, of which maybe two-thirds will be peasants and proletarians. All of our health developments except birth control programs go in the direction of increasing these numbers. However, until recently we have spent annually—we in all the world— less than 100 million dollars on birth control programs. Basically, for peasants and for ourselves, we have the alternative of maintaining what health we have and protecting it, or of allowing famine to develop. The Population Crisis Committee, The United Nations and its special agencies, the major foundations, and finally the United States government have gotten involved in population programs. These are perhaps capable of protecting a part of the health of peasants.

In the final analysis we have the choice between highly organized planning to maintain widespread quasi-health or the alternative of famine. It may already be too late to avert the starvation of tens of millions in the 1970's and 1980's. Hunger is not exactly a disease, but for most of the world's population it is a constant condition. "As healthy as a peasant" means suffering most of the time, as opposed to "as healthy as a suburbanite" which means living a well-protected, comfortable, and long life. Yet for all of this striving it must be realized that health is no panacea. Dubos observes that health is important, but "Human life implies adventure, and there is no adventure without struggles and dangers" (Dubos, 1959). It is no cultural accident that "to your health" is a common toast among urbanites as well as peasants.

MARY W. HELMS

Peasants & Purchasers: Preliminary Thoughts on a Differentiation of Intermediate Societies

In the literature on "post-contact" cultures there is a noticeable trend to classify groups either as broken remnants of past aboriginal societies or as lying somewhere on a one-way street from "tribal" to "peasant" to "urban" (or "modern"). That such a line of development does exist is obvious; that it is so direct or straightforward is open to question, since the term "peasant" traditionally has been used in a restricted sense to refer to largely self-sufficient rural agriculturalists tied to an agrarian state (cf. Foster 1967:4-6). Only if "peasantry" is defined much more broadly can *all* nonprimitive, nonmodern societies be included. This is one possibility. Yet to extend the definition may be to include so much cultural diversity under a single term that it would become much too general, losing much of its heuristic value (cf. Halpern and Brode 1967:51). The other possibility would be to limit the application of "peasantry" to a narrower range of culture patterns. This, in fact, seems to be the approach most often used. But to follow a restricted definition of "peasant" implies that there may well be intermediate societies falling outside the classification.

This paper suggests a category of nonprimitive, nonmodern society other than peasantry in order to delineate further an increasingly useful definition of "peasantry," and also to provide a general framework within which a number of intermediate societies might fit. A detailed systematic analysis (through cross-cultural comparison) of the criteria which characterize this category is beyond the scope of this paper. Here we merely wish to suggest some guidelines for future investigations.

It is occasionally noted in the literature that the rise of civilizations or states has transformed primitive peoples into a number of "other types." For example, Redfield, in his classic discussion of peasantry, takes fleeting note of the existence of various frontier societies which resemble the peasantry in some respects but which are unlike them in others (1956:20-21; see also 1953:29, 44-45). Similarly, Casagrande speaks briefly of *"multifarious* types of societies that stand in this middle range between the relatively self-contained tribal group . . . on the one hand and the urbanized center, metropolitan community, nation, state, or civilization on the other . . . ." (1959:2; italics mine). More specifically, Lehman has proposed a category distinct from both tribal and peasant cultures to provide a framework for analyzing certain Southeast Asian mountain-dwelling societies (1963:224-5).

In addition to consideration of typology, there are a number of ethnographic monographs documenting specific cultural patterns which are not primitive but to which the term "peasant" is not generally applied. For example, there are studies of hunting and gathering peoples of Alaska and Canada who have adapted to the fur trade and to wage labor (Leacock, 1954; VanStone, 1962, 1965). Similar accounts of Amazon Basin cultures, such as the Mundurucu and the Tenetehara, describe groups which prepared manioc flour, sarsaparilla, palm oils and other forest products for exchange with Brazilian traders, and who also became involved in the fluctuations of a boom-and-bust rubber economy (Murphy 1960; Wagley and Galvao 1949).

There are also many societies in the highlands of Southeast Asia which are not generally considered to be peasants. These include groups such as the Chin, who traded jungle products or labor for prestige items and iron tools from neighboring Burma, or the Lamet of northern Laos who raised rice for sale and engaged in wage labor in Thailand to obtain pottery, iron goods, cloth and cash (Lehman 1963; Izikowitz 1951).

My own investigations among the Miskito of eastern Nicaragua, who grow rice and beans, cut chicle or lumber, seek work in gold mines to acquire a wide range of foreign goods did not reveal a peasant society (Helms 1967). Furthermore, it is difficult to construe such cultures as being tribal or primitive since they, and undoubtedly many like them, have been involved (often for centuries) with large, complex systems of a far different order from anything usually encountered in the primitive world. Even more important, these societies have positively adapted to the outside world in order to form a culture pattern which is neither primitive nor peasant-like in its overall configurations (cf. Murphy and Steward 1956).

What is the nature of this adaptation? How does it contrast with that made by peasant societies which are also linked by definition with a larger system? The essential points for comparison would seem to lie in the character of the involvement with the outside world. Like peasantry, "purchasers," as we shall call these societies, interact with a wider society by producing goods and services for this society, but for different reasons and in a different way. It is incumbent upon the peasant to produce an excess above and beyond that amount required for his household's needs or, alternately, to step down his own needs in order to have an available surplus. This is because peasants are subject to a superior outside power-holder who requires the payment of some sort of "rent" such as labor, produce, or money (Wolf 1966:9-10, 15).

In contrast, the interaction between purchasers and the outside world is characterized not by an asymmetrical flow of payments to central authorities, but by a balance of trade. Besides local, essentially traditional subsistence activities, local products or labor are exchanged in a quite symmetrical fashion for foreign material goods—salt, flour, clothing, iron tools, etc., which have become essentials of daily life. This is not to say that peasants do not trade. The point is that peasants also have another demand placed upon their production—that of providing various rents to the state—which purchasers effectively avoid. Also unlike peasantry, purchasers may engage in pursuits other than agriculture—fishing, hunting, collecting natural resources, or wage labor to fulfill their role in the wider economy. Therefore, purchase societies may be found in relation to industrial (or industrializing) as well as non-industrial states, whereas by most definitions peasants are a feature only of the latter.

The fundamental difference between these two systems can be examined from a number of other viewpoints. One approach might focus on the sources of personal motivation for interaction with the larger society. The peasant, being subject to the wishes of an overlord, *must,* regardless of other obligations, forfeit a certain amount of time, labor or produce to the state. The purchaser, on the other hand, has greater flexibility and may contribute the amount of materials or time as he sees fit. One example, the unreliable native laborer who works only when he wishes and for as long as he wishes has often been noted in the literature. Even taking credit systems into account, we will venture the generalization that it is primarily when salt or sugar or a new axe is needed that a man will go to the bush to cut chicle, or seek work at a mine, or trap furs. In other words, the *extent to which foreign items are desired,* rather than the necessity of paying rents, is the major factor governing the degree to which trade or labor occurs between purchase societies and the wider world. Of course, the introduction of foreign goods and the subsequent development of purchase societies often stemmed from the foreign society's desire for local products, and in this sense the forces which moved the once self-sufficient native culture into a more complex economy also came from outside. But once foreign items became necessary for daily life, they were sought by the natives of their own accord.

Credit systems tend to be seen as harshly controlling and exploitative by definition. The "classic case" which generally comes to mind in the economic frontiers with which we are concerned is the situation at the height of the rubber trade in the Amazon Basin, which did employ harsh methods to keep collectors at work. But this may be an extreme example. It is also possible to find examples of harried traders trying to cope with the inconsistent tastes of their native clients, or helpless to collect back debts. The credit system is probably more severe than anything found in the primitive world, yet in general it seems to permit more maneuvering on the part of the purchaser than state controls do on the part of the peasantry. Under any conditions, credit systems are basically symmetrical arrangements of exchange (even if the purchasing portion occurs prior to payment), whereas demands upon the peasantry are more asymmetrical since they are part of (and thus legitimately backed by) the power structure of the state.

In order to establish the necessary economic ties, a number of changes may occur within the once primitive culture. Social organization or social relationships may need to be altered in order to permit (or give priority to) the wider economic interest; political allegiances may shift, and world view may adjust (cf. Murphy and Steward 1956). In all these areas, it is valid to search for similarities and differences not only between various purchase societies, but also between purchasers and peasants (as well as between primitives and purchasers). One example of the contrasts may be found in the different world views of purchasers and peasants. Peasants appear to be characterized by a general hesitancy to become too involved with the outside world (Wolf *op. cit.*, p. 16). A fear of new things, of becoming too committed to the offerings of the larger society seems to correlate with the peasant's problem of having to meet both the demands of the state and his family's personal wants. One way of handling these opposing forces is to minimize personal wants by avoiding the temptations of new things. Purchasers, on the other hand, who do not have damaging political ties but who maintain potentially gainful economic relationships with the outside world, have nothing to gain and, in fact, much to lose, by attenuating outside channels. Consequently, a desire for gain, an attitude of interest in, and positive orientation toward the outside world may be generally characteristic of purchasers. Such, at any rate, was the attitude I found during my own fieldwork among the Miskito (Helms *op. cit.*, p. 395ff).

In summary, I have suggested that, in addition to peasantry, there is a category of intermediate society articulated with the outside world through particular economic ties in such a way that a positive adaptation to the larger ssytem results. The exact nature of this adaptation, its structural similarities to and differences from other intermediate societies, as well as primitive cultures, have not been adequately analyzed on a cross-cultural basis; but this would seem to be a fruitful direction for further, more detailed investigations.

E. A. HAMMEL

The "Balkan" Peasant: A View from Serbia

Several generations of anthropological research have demonstrated that the description of a culture area is not an easy task,
largely because of the difficulties of determining its boundaries.
Just as in physical anthropology, where the mapping of racial
characteristics usually can only provide a description of overlap-
ping continuous distributions, or in dialectography, where the
mapping of linguistic differences most often yields dialect areas of
gradual differentiation, so also do general cultural descriptions of
an area present a complex mosaic of traits which gradually change
across the landscape. We can, of course, describe these changes in
isolating terms, just as students of human biology specify the clines
of differentiation in blood type, or as the linguists draw their
isoglosses and note major breaks in distribution in their isogloss
bundles. But as the number of traits observed increases to the point
where cultural description becomes interesting and satisfying, the
neatness of the differentiations across the land in any transect melts
into confusion. The spatial distributions of a series of discrete cultural traits over large areas tend to independence and noncongru-
ence.

One of the solutions to this descriptive problem has been to concern ourselves more with the centers of areas than with their
peripheries, that is with the points where sets of important cultural
variables intersect. Thus, the high cultures of South America are

conceived of as having a center in the Andes around Cuzco, those of Middle America in the Valley of Mexico or in Guatemala or Yucatan, with the realization that geographical distantiation from those centers involves a gradual tapering off of the unique intersections that characterize the cultures at the centers, which are thought to be typical.

The use of the Central American example indicates that both the typicality and the location of the center shift through time; the nature and the locus of Olmec culture, of Old Empire Maya, and of Central America of the "Mexican" period differ. That situation is particularly acute when the locus itself is selected as the primary point of reference in description, rather than concentrating on the ebb and flow of complexes which change their central loci even if their natures remain similar. In this context, it seems useful to ask: Just what do we mean by the "Balkan peasant"?

With a few exceptions, the Balkan area is meaningful as a culture area more because of its equidistance from centers of other typical cultural complexes than as the locus of some independent cultural climax which influenced its neighbors. Through most of history, the Balkans have been a nadir rather than a zenith of cultural developments, or at least a conduit through which cultural innovations in other areas have passed. About five thousand years before Christ, the first agricultural practices crept up the Danube and along the Vardar-Morava corridor from the Near East to Central Europe. Later, the bronze of the Near East, and still later the iron of Anatolia forged new pathways to the north and west. With the Indo-European invasions, the Illyrians and Thracians penetrated, only to be isolated (we think) in the mountain fastness of present Albania. The Celts swept through, and the ancestors of the Greeks on their way to the conquest of Minoan Crete. The Romans marched across to their last frontier in Dacia and a secondary locus of empire in Constantinople. It is with this last development that the stage was set for the modern Balkan era, in which the historical conduit became pinched at both ends by developing empires which vied against one another and squeezed the Balkans like a kernel in the multiple jaws of a nutcracker. From the development of Rome as the first Western power, its Drang nach Osten, the development of Byzantium and the surging tides of barbarians from the steppes, the Balkans have been a battleground and an area of refuge.

The Slavs first crossed the Danube into the Balkans about A.D. 500 as part of the barbarian wave, but by the ninth century they were caught between the continuing pressures from the east and new ones developing from the west. Those who penetrated into the Alps were conquered by the Franks who, after Charlemagne, were laying the foundations of modern central Europe. From the east, in the ninth century, the Magyars poured over the Carpathians to exert continued pressure, with the Germans, on the Croats. From the southeast, the Byzantine remnants of Rome pushed up the Danube basin. The struggle for territory and power was ideologically symbolized and formalized in the contest between the Papacy and the church of Constantinople, so that those Slavs under Germanic and Magyar influence came to be Roman Catholics and those under Byzantium to be Orthodox. With the Ottoman conquest of Byzantium, Islam continued the northwestward battle, squeezing the Orthodox against the Roman and converting many to itself. Later, the Slavic peoples were trapped between the Germans and the Hungarians on one front, the Turks on a second, and the Venetians on a third. Still later, they were caught between the Soviet Union and the loose federation of the Western powers. Incumbents change, but the roles seem to go on forever.

One might guess from all of this that the culture of the Balkans would show no individuality of its own, that it would be a dark and bloody ground showing only the footprints of recent conquerors. Indeed, it was a bloody ground (and is, and may yet be), and it does show the traces of many passages, but it also demonstrates a stubborn retention of ancient legacy and a unique and innovative combination of influences.

We have only to turn to political history to see that the Slavs were not passive material for conquest. They have never been an easy morsel for the Germans and Magyars to digest, and Croatian pressures for trialism in the Austro-Hungarian Empire were strong and important. To the southeast, the medieval kingdom of Serbia in the fourteenth century rivalled the weakening Byzantium and contributed to its decline. Ragusa (now Dubrovnik) maintained a clever independence both from Turks and Venetians, achieving a powerful position of its own until it finally fell to the French. The Turkish conquest of the Balkans was no easy task, either. After the initial strategic victory of the Ottomans in 1371 at the Maritsa, it was almost two decades until the final defeat of the Serbian state at Kosovo (1389) and over a hundred-thirty until the conquest of Belgrade. From the early seventeenth until the twentieth century, Slavic troops held the line against Turkey in their capacity as Austrian border forces, and their fellows under Turkish control threw off the yoke, at least temporarily, in 1804. A second revolt succeeded in 1814, and with various guarantees and assistance from the European powers and Russia, the Serbs pushed the Turks to final defeat in 1912. After the defeat of the Austro-Hungarian Empire, in which the Serbs participated, the multinational Kingdom of the Serbs, Croats and Slovenes enjoyed a mildly successful political existence until it suffered a second defeat at German hands in World War II. The resistance movement of Jugoslavia during the Second World War is a classic in the annals of peasant rebellion; like few such rebellions, it succeeded, and like still fewer it succeeded with little outside help. But within a decade of success, the internationalist Communist ideology, which had apparently motivated it, yielded to the underlying fires of nationalism, and the political position of the modern state is again that of subtle mediation between opposing Goliaths. One is reminded not only of Dubrovnik between the Venetians and the Turks, or the Serbs between them and the Austrians, but of the Jews between Egypt and Babylon and the Cambodians between the Thais and the Vietnamese.

In other areas of culture, one finds the same picture of independence, dependence, and mediation. The Slovenes have maintained their own language and literature under German domination for a thousand years, and Slovenian dialects are still spoken even in Austrian Carniola. Similarly, there are Slavic speakers in Greece, in Albania, and part of Italy. At the same time, Slavic speakers within Jugoslvia are often bilingual, and their dialects show heavy influences from neighboring languages. German is a useful language in Slovenia, Italian in Dalmatia, and Turkish is still spoken in some regions. Peasant costume is a blend of former styles of empires, and the cuisine of any area is a patchwork of the menus of conquerors. One has only to observe the cavalry-like breeches of Serbian peasants, the harem trousers of Bosnian women, the sandals with turned-up toes, to eat the pastries of Zagreb or the grilled meats and cabbage rolls of Serbia, to drink the wine of Dalmatia or the thick coffee of Bosnia. In music, only the keenest Arab ear can distinguish between the dances of Kosovo-Metohija and those of Iraq, while the mixed-part singing of Slovenia sounds like an Austrian boys' choir and its dance tunes like the Schuhplatte. But some things are mixed, like the open-throat singing of some Serbian songs while others are sung in tense, Middle-Eastern style. Others are unique, like the magnificent epic poetry which so inspired Goethe.

In all this variety, in all this blending and interinfluence, where does one find an anchor point? Inevitably, it is at those points least affected by the political control of competing empires, those farthest removed from mercantile influence and other contacts, those areas of refuge in which the more indigenous (or at least the older foreign) elements were able to develop as independently as culture ever develops. There is no such thing as a "Balkan peasant"; rather there are many kinds including a few which are as little like their neighbors as it is possible to be. Those further from the center of the refuge area are progressively more like Italian peasants, or Greek, or Turkish or Hungarian or German ones, although they continue to share many of the traits of those in the center, such as language, music and art styles, and features of economic and social organization.

This negative center of gravity is located in eastern Montenegro and eastern Herzegovina, and in the adjoining areas of western Serbia. We might include Albania except for the fact that its language differs so sharply and that we really know too little about it in detail. Although Montenegro was "conquered" by the Turks, they controlled but little of it, and their hold on the adjoining mountains of eastern Herzegovina was about as slim. As they retreated, it was into western Serbia that the pursuing Slavs spread, so that in that general area of Nikšić to Užice and Valjevo and to the Bosnian border, the area of least foreign influence has had the longest life-span. Linguistically, the central area is characterized by a relatively uniform dialect, the jekavian variant of the štokavina, which was utilized by the grammarian Karadžić in his reform of the Serbian language in the early nineteenth century. (Karadžić's father came from the area of Šavnik in eastern Herzegovina and he himself was born in Tržić in western Serbia.) Economically, it is not a rich area; the higher reaches of the mountains are suitable only for grazing, mostly of sheep and goats; some potatoes and grains are grown lower down the slopes, and fruits are widely cultivated, usually for making brandies. In recent years, industry has penetrated the area, and vigorous provincial towns have grown where only market centers existed before. Mining is still important in parts of the region, an activity that goes back to the Middle Ages. In general, however, it is poor, backward, and peopled by stubbornly independent mountaineers.

When the Slavs first came into the Balkans, they were a nomadic people, probably practicing a combination of herding and shifting cultivation. Their social organization was probably structured along patrilineal lines, with patrilocal postmarital residence, and the kinship terminology was most likely of an approximate Omaha type (Freidrich 1962; Hammel 1957, MSa). In this they differ very little from most pre-modern Indo-Europeans; for example, the early Roman kinship terminology had similar features, and the agnatic corporacy of its kin groups is well known (Lounsbury, 1964). Those Slavs who settled in the more fertile and outlying areas of the region underwent a series of changes both as a result of a changed economic system and of cultural influence from their neighbors. Those who settled, or were pushed into, less hospitable and more remote areas retained these ancient traits in greater degree. In fact, it was as refugees that the Balkan Slavs developed a social organization almost unique in modern Europe, one matched only by that of the Albanians whom the Slavs had pushed ahead of them into what Coon has called the "eagle rookery" of Europe (Coon 1950). It would be a mistake, I think, to regard this social organization merely as a survival of ancient forms, persisting intact except for the stripping away of earlier elaborations. More likely, it was a synthesis of organizational principles available under the old system, with particular features emphasized by ecological and political conditions.

In its general outlines, this Dinaric social structure was a fragile tissue of patrilineal organization, based on a minimal lineage called the "house" (kućá) (Hammel MSa). Membership in the house was ordinarily restricted to a man, his wife, his unmarried daughters, his sons, and their wives and unmarried children. It might include his married grandsons, or from their point of view it might include patrilateral parallel first cousins, but the house usually divided before that stage of growth. The separate nuclear families of such a house usually had separate hearths, and the house was referred to as one of so many "smokes" or "hearths" or "pothook chains." These hearths were sometimes simply laid out along the major axis of the building, and as the membership grew, so did the length of the house by extension of the long walls; often partitions were erected between the separate hearths.

The members of a house thus had a common residence but separate control of consumption. They herded their cattle together when it was convenient to do so, but maintained separate ownership. When a son married, he received his portion of his father's herd and set up his own hearth, tended by his new wife. When the father died, or when the grandchildren reached maturity, the household usually split up, some of the brothers remaining in the vicinity but others perhaps moving tens or hundreds of miles away. Frequently, members of the household, or the entire household fled the area because of blood guilt and the ensuing feud. Often they were pushed from their land in the Balkan equivalent of range wars, as more powerful groups of agnates displaced them. Usually, these pressures came from the lowlands, as other Slavs were displaced up the slopes by Turkish or other pressure; when that pressure slackened, the mountaineers flowed back down the slopes in search of more fertile lands.

Patrilineal kinship was important far beyond the household and formed the base for the tribal political system. Closely related houses, for example those standing in the relation of patrilateral first or second cousins, formed lineages of middle range, called "families" (*porodice*). At even wider ranges, agnates formed "brotherhoods" (*bratstva*), in which the lineal reckoning often ran twelve to fourteen generations deep. These brotherhoods were, effectively, maximal lineages, although several brotherhoods might assume putative agnatic relationship on some other grounds, such as a common name or common religious cult. Brotherhoods were grouped into "tribes" (*plemena*), which were united through a formal system of offices, use of a common territory and natural resources, and the existence of an institutionalized means for the settlement of blood feuds. Although there were higher levels of political organization, such as the *nahija,* these were administrative-territorial units imposed by would-be conquerors such as the Turks or the King of Montenegro, none of which was very successful in subjugating or unifying the region in a stable fashion.

The corporacy and solidarity of these agnatic units are visible in other ways. Naming patterns emphasized patrilineal descent and membership in an agnatic group. A man's first name was that given to him at baptism, his second name was a patronymic based on the baptismal name of his father, and his third name was a patronymic based on the baptismal name of his paternal grandfather. Since the cycle of linege fission at the lower levels was a short one, the grand-parental name often served as a group name as well as an individu-al one. In addition, men might have still another name based on the baptismal name of the founding ancestor of their *bratstvo*, or they might use that name rather than the grandparental one. The names derived from the identity of a founding ancestor were sel-dom used as individual identifiers in the home area; to draw a linguistically familiar example, everyone in the house would know who Olaf was, unless there were two, and then it was enough to refer to Olaf Eriksson. That device was also sufficient outside the house, unless one were far from home or there were several Olaf Erikssons in the neighborhood, in which case accurate reference would have to make use of the fact that Erik was Erik Svensson. But in the Scandinavian example, there was no group called "Erikssons" or "Svenssons" in a *formal* sense. In the Montenegrin case, Sava Djurov was Sava, the son of Djuro, Djuro was Djuro Jankov, the son of Janko, and all were Janković, which was a *group*.

Religious observances also played a symbolic role. The Serbs and Montenegrins observe a household feast in honor of a particular saint, on whose day the founder of the family was supposed to have been converted to Christianity. From this it follows that agnates will have the same household feast, or *slava*. The converse of that proposition, that all persons having the same *slava* were agnates, was often the base for acknowledgement of putative kin-ship linkage. The name, of course, was used in the same way, so that two men who were both Jankovici but strangers to one an-other might assume that they were kin and treat each other ac-cordingly. Unmarried men and women, meeting in a strange market, might assume that they were not eligible spouses if they had the same name and *slava*, even though they had no direct knowledge of their kinship connections. As lineages grew in depth and span, kinship linkages weakened, and segments of growing independence might forget their ultimate founding ancestors and begin to reckon from another at the point of effective fission from their former kinsmen; the name of that founding ancestor became the name of the group. The epitome of this situation is when men begin to use the names of their paternal grandfathers exclusively as group names, so that the agnatic group contains only first cousins. Just as fission led to the adoption of new names, it also led to the adoption of new household feasts which symbolized the separation of lineage segments.

The "natural" developmental cycle of these lineages was one of fission. However, lineages often fused. In the commonest occurrence, related segments of a lineage or the several lineages of a brotherhood, or the several brotherhoods of a tribe, drew together to face a common enemy, either in defense or in offense. This kind of fusion was of course most common at lower lineage levels, and the solidarity of a tribe was an ephemeral thing. In other instances, however, nonagnates were adopted into an agnatic group. Adoption of unrelated individuals was the lowest-order example of this process, in which an unrelated person could be brought into a house and treated as a brother whereupon he took the name of the house and its *slava*. At higher levels, a weak and unprotected household could obtain the protection of a brotherhood by adopting its name and *slava*. Whole lineages could be adopted by others in this way. There were two very common circumstances leading to individual and group adoption. In the first, a father with no sons might marry one of his daughters to a man who would live in the family of his bride, departing from the usual rule of patrivirilocality. The groom, called *uljez* (from the verb "to intrude") or *domazet* ("son-in-law of the house"), might take on his father-in-law's name and would certainly celebrate the *slava* of his bride's family, either in addition to his own or solely. In the second circumstance, an agnatic group fleeing its old precincts would invariably seek some local alliance where it chose to settle. That alliance might be arranged through marriage or ritual ties, but often came about through outright adoption, with assumption of the name or *slava* of the dominant group, or both.

Further evidence of the importance of agnatic grouping and household structure can be seen in the kinship terminology (Hammel 1957, MSa). Modern Serbian and Montenegrin terminology does not have the Omaha structure that the system of the earliest Slavs may have had, but it has numerous features which reflect the agnatic emphasis of the social organization. A man's brother's son, for example, is called by a term (*sinovac*) based on the lexical root for "son" (*sin*). A man's brother's son will eventually share in the resources controlled by himself and his brother (particularly when the extended family is a powerful social unit), while a sister's son will not. Sister's sons are called by a diminutive of the term for sister, and women use a diminutive of the word for brother to name their brother's sons. Thus, the peculiar term for sibling's child is restricted to the nephews of men, in accord with the social situation. One's aunts are not distinguished in the terminology; both are called by the same term. On the other hand, the two uncles are separated; in this we see a reflection of the fact that aunts have no share in inheritance nor are they coresident after their marriage, while the father's brother has a peculiar position in an agnatic system which is recognized in the terminology. Of course, this situation mirrors the use of a special term for a man's brother's son.

In the terminology for relatives by marriage, *zet* referred to sister's husband, daughter's husband, and husband's sister's husband—in other words, *zet* was a man who took a bride from one's household. *Snaha* referred to brother's wife and son's wife, and at more extended ranges to the wife of *sinovac* (a man's nephew)—in other words, all those young women who joined one's household. The women who married a set of brothers and who would thus live with or very close to one another had a mutual term of reference based on a Slavic root (*jetrva*), whereas the men who married a set of sisters and who would have little or nothing to do with one another had only a borrowed term of Turkish origin.

Nowhere is the agnatic basis of social organization clearer than in the institution of the blood feud. When homicide occurred, the *lex talionis* was invoked, and the feud might involve whole brotherhoods, although usually in a series of snipings rather than battles. The closest agnates of a murdered man were bound to avenge him, although a proud and courageous widow might do so herself. Similarly, if the murderer himself could not be found, his closest agnates might be killed in revenge. The feud could be settled in a variety of ways—through payment of blood money, perhaps by marriage, and most typically by calling into play the institution of ritual sponsorship at the baptism of a child. By offering a child to be baptized by the kin of the murdered man, the murderer and his family would beg forgiveness, and the feud might end. Since the relationship of godfather to godchild was a *group* relationship, ideally inherited in the male line, such a contract might lead to a long-lasting bond between two groups, as another thread in the social fabric otherwise bound only by agnation and marriage (Hammel MSa).

As the Turk loosened his hold on the Balkans, beginning in the late eighteenth century, the tribes that had been bottled up in the Dinaric fastness rolled down the slopes, worrying his heels and stabbing at his flanks. In an extraordinary series of migrations, the Slavs reclaimed the land from which they had been ousted over the preceding three or four centuries. The forward move was one of predatory lineage expansion, facilitated by the existing agnatic structure and emphasizing certain of its details. (Sahlins 1961). With new land available, the fission of lineages proceeded apace, households streaming out to carve new homesteads from a fertile oak wilderness which had been largely ignored by the town-dwelling Turk, and from which the Slavs had earlier fled to avoid him. At the same time, the richness of the land made it possible to remain longer, and in larger household groups, in one location. Intensive grain cultivation, combined with commercial raising of pigs fattened on the abundant acorns, replaced dependence on sheep and goats. The household grew in size, consolidating its power and holdings, but the extensive character of the migrations destroyed the superordinate structure of brotherhoods and tribes. Rather, there came into existence a village organization based on large extended households bound together by contractual political ties. For a time, the new structure existed under an umbrella of remaining Turkish overlordship (but one devoid of much of its former power), and in the nineteenth century the Karadjordjević and Obrenović dynasties took over the reins, competing with each other for power.

These new, large households were run as family corporations in which adult male members had joint shares, without much status distinction, until the household broke up. Publicized by pan-Slavism and early socialist writings, this household unit, the *zadruga,* became a classic example of peasant communism, on a par with the Russian *mir.* A *zadruga* might have as many as a hundred members under the same roof or at least within the same complex of buildings. Its work was presided over by the senior male, usually the father or elder brother or the eldest of a set of parallel cousins. He usually held his post by virtue of age and kinship rank, but achievement within this ascriptive framework was not uncommon, so that capable men were often elected and retained by their housemates (Tomasic 1948). Normally, the wife of the head man (who was himself called *starešina*—the "old man") oversaw the domestic arrangements, commanding the corps of sons' and brothers' and cousins' wives. Labor was finely divided, with some men responsible for craft work, others for stock-raising, others for growing grain, and so on. A large household often had but a single hearth, all the men eating in common, followed by their wives and children. Married couples, particularly the younger ones, usually had separate sleeping quarters in small huts arranged around the main house, or they had separate rooms in the main house. Often, when the winters were severe, married couples had their own room during the snows but stayed in a cabin in the summer. It was also common for the household to have lowland and upland loci; part of the family stayed in the valley in the summer, while the younger folk went to the mountains to tend the herds and pasture the swine. Very large households might have two separate major residences, sometimes separated by many miles.

In these two comparisons, between the Montenegrin and the Serbian social organizations, we can see the importance of several variables: the fertility and availability of land, the mobility of the population, and the locus and strength of superordinate political power. In the refuge areas of Montenegro, land was infertile but abundant. Most of the economy was based on herding, which demanded at least seasonal mobility, and the nature of the pastures called for relatively small social groups. At the same time, the unstable political situation and feuding precluded the formation of large, stable, joint-families. The agnatic group with common residence was thus fragile, predisposed to quick fission and the out-migration of its segments. Balancing this fragility, however, were the ties of kinship, marriage, and ritual relations which facilitated cooperation, channelled feuding, and allowed for the fusion of segments at ever higher levels. Superordinate political power was sufficiently weak and distant to allow the agnatic principle to work as a political dimension almost to the level of the tribe, and the entire structure was one well suited to an uncertain and migratory situation which called for rapid recombinations of social groupings (cf. Murphy and Kasdan, 1959).

In the more fertile lowland areas, larger groups could be supported at a given locus, so that the household could increase in membership. At the same time, the dangerous conditions of pioneer existence required a goodly number of males on one homestead, and the combination of transhumant herding and farming called for a population large enough to assume the separate labors and manage the affairs of the peasant corporation. However, there were no political pressures from within to require the extension of kinship principles into the upper reaches of political organization. As the Slavs followed the Turkish retreat, the scope of their migrations became sufficiently large to preclude large-scale agnatic organization, because of the mixture of population, and they were forever moving onward. The institutions of political coordination that arose were contractual and restricted to the village level. Often, the Slavs came into areas that were not completely free of Turkish control but simply under nominal control, and that factor also precluded the growth of strong political organizations above the village level. By the time the Turk had finally been removed, the growth of a Serbian dynasty again prevented the emergence of an agnatically-based tribal structure. This is not to say that agnatic kinship was not important in the village or that households were not agnatically related. In point of fact, villages were usually composed of agnatic clusters, each of which might contain a number of large households. The clusters came into being simply because brothers and cousins tended to build their houses close to one another after division of a joint household, if they stayed in the general area at all. Thus, in a Serbian village the households were larger and the lineages smaller in span than in Montenegro, and the contractual ties of the Serbian village paralleled those of the Montenegrin tribe.

Under different social conditions, the household and kinship organization were again different. On the Miltary Border of Croatia, along which many Serbs were employed as border guards by the Austro-Hungarian Monarchy, the *zadruga* became a very large and important social unit, elaborated and formalized to a degree unknown elsewhere. The land was sufficiently fertile to support large units, and the population sufficiently immobile to allow households to grow to a size of as much as 100. Further, the policies of the Monarchy encouraged the formation of joint-households in order to provide a basis for conscription without seriously interfering with the peasant economy.

In Southern Serbia the situation was quite different. Land was scarce, the control of the Turk was still firm, and there were already rather large Slavic populations settled on the land in serf-like status. The growth of large households was precluded by the scarcity of land, as was the formation of agnatic clusters, and Turkish control was strong and near enough to prevent the formation of any autonomous political institutions.

These features of social and political organization persisted until just before World War I. In the areas that had long been free of effective Turkish control but which held large populations on fertile land, population expansion on limited land, combined with usurious lending practices, led to the ruin of many peasant families. By the end of World War I, the emphasis on a money economy began to chip away at the foundations of family corporacy, and the institution of equal inheritance rights for women destroyed the legitimation of effective agnatic control. These changes were accelerated between the two wars, leading to a decline of the *zadruga* as an institution. At the same time, however, lowered mortality rates led to an increase in the *size* of joint-households, if not in their lateral kinship span. Most of the increase can be attributed to the gradual aging of the population and the delay in fission is thus attributable to the later death of the founder and a longer developmental cycle (Halpern and Anderson MS.). Political control by the central government increased, so that village institutions were subsumed under a state structure, and the wide-ranging agnatic networks of Montenegro and Herzegovina lost their political efficacy. Overall demographic statistics which concentrate on family size thus do not give an accurate picture of household composition; more detailed analyses show the acceleration in the rate of fission of households and the stretching out of laterally extended joint families into lineally extended ones (Halpern and Anderson MS.; Mosely 1040, 1943, 1953; Hammel MSa).

Since World War II, even more profound changes have altered the society and culture of the Jugoslav peasant. Unlike the earlier ones, these seem more evenly distributed across the Balkan area (with the exception of Albania), and Jugoslavia in fact is now more of a positive center than at any time since the twelfth century. The success of the peasant revolution, largely on its own terms, and the commitment of the new Jugoslav state to industrialization and federalism have pushed the twentieth century directly into a countryside that might have otherwise remained (and might have wished to remain) in the nineteenth. Although there are a number of large industrial centers, there are also many provincial ones, and the articulation of peasant life with the national scene is growing ever closer (Halpern 1965). These changes have resulted from three phenomena: the migration of peasants to urban centers, the employment of rural-dwelling peasants in provincial industry, and the penetration of urban culture to the countryside by mere propinquity or through the mass media.

Before World War II, 80% of the Jugoslav population was engaged in agriculture, and now the figure stands at less than 50%. From 1945 to the present, great numbers of people left the countryside for the towns and cities, at rates as high as 380,000 per year (Hoffman and Neal 1952:485). In 1921, 9% of the population lived in cities of 20,000 or more inhabitants, but by 1960 the figure was 20% (SFRJ 1948, 1955, 1961). These massive shifts did much to reduce the agricultural overpopulation of the country, which stood at about 35% in the 1930's, but they do not tell the whole story (Sentić and Obradović 1963:311). The out-migration of younger people, particularly males, was heavier than that of other persons, so that villages now have an older population than before (Livada 1966). At the same time, many people who remained in the village are now working in occupations outside agriculture. For centuries, some rural dwellers participated in mining, and that continues. However, an increasing number work in provincial industries, returning to their farms in the evening or on weekends (Kostić 1955, 1959). Many farm families have found a means of survival in this day of cash economy through the employment of some of their sons in local industry, and the early stages of industrialization have strengthened the patrilocal extended family where the father's authority is still strong.

At the same time, many peasants on the periphery of cities and towns have shifted to a market-oriented agriculture, growing food for the increasing urban population. It is not an uncommon sight in the villages outside Belgrade to see peasants boarding the bus with a load of produce to sell in the city markets, or even loading up their own automobiles to transport their products. Those who live farther away often send a family member to live in the city during the harvest season, shiping produce to him by rail. Even those who sell to agricultural cooperatives or provincial buyers are now more closely tied to the urban system than they were before.

As in other developing countries, the advent of electrification and battery-powered radios has brought much of the city into the countryside. Further, the Jugoslavs are a nation of newspaper readers, so that urban culture has an even greater penetration. Those peasants who are illiterate, as 25% of them are, (Magner 1967) can at least listen to the radio, or hear their neighbors relate the events in the papers, and some of them can even watch television.

There is, however, an important factor in the transmission of culture from the city to the countryside that shows a marked difference from the historical situation: that to the peasant the cities are now *his* cities. Under the Turk and the Austrian, the cities were the loci of foreign power and by and large of foreign population. Now they are full of peasants like himself, or at least of people whose fathers were peasants. Today, the peasant can prize the values of the city without totally negating his own culture. There is a great disdain for many of the aspects of peasant life, strongly felt among urbanites and growing stronger among peasants, but the disdain is not a total one. No longer is farming thought of as the best or the most secure occupation: the more interesting jobs in industry as well as ideological pressure on the peasantry have seen to that. Further, the material benefits—in higher wages, more varied food, cinema, and just cultural variety and liveliness—are a powerful magnet drawing peasants to the city. But in some ways the old distrust of the city—of civilization—lingers. If the peasant is regarded as a brute "man with the hoe," if his illiteracy merits contempt, if his disregard of sanitation and his work habits attuned to the seasons rather than the time clock call down upon him the epithets reserved for Southern Negroes in the United States, he retains a peculiar moral superiority. With a history of foreign domination and an oral literature of underground resistance, the peasant is the embodiment of the nation as a concept, the soul of the people as a body (Halpern and Hammel MS).

From time to time, one meets an old peasant in the village, or worse yet in the city—drunk, dishevelled, smelling of garlic and week-old sweat, and with the noon's *musaka* still clinging to his moustaches. He will begin to tell you about his life—as a child, he guarded the sheep from wolves and carried newborn lambs to the fold; in 1912, he fought the Turks barehanded down the Vardar corridor; in 1915, he struggled with Durkheim's son through the passes of Albania to Corfu; in 1918, he was a *Solunac*—one of those who drove the Germans from Salonika to Belgrade in six weeks, in a military advance that was paralleled only by Patton in World War II (Adams 1949:90-91); from 1942 to 1945, he carried out (whether a Partizan or a Chetnik) the most difficult peasant guerilla campaign the West has known, equalled only by the Long March of the Chinese or the struggles of the Viet Minh and Viet Cong. Then he went back to the rocky soil of Valjevo to grow his plums, and make his brandy, and to father yet another brood. As he tells this, his watery eyes clear, the trembling hands take on the look of old oak, the voice firms, the trochaic meter of the epics beats a line as his story blends with that of Kosovo, and the aorist and imperfective and other forgotten tenses of Indo-European play against one another. Sons-in-law look embarassed, grandchildren look bored, sons and daughters are indulgent of the old man's prattling, but to the romantic ethnographer's eyes, the old man grows like Jack's beanstalk. And when this seeps through to the family, their urban facade fades, eyes soften, and they honor the old man for what he was and for what the nation may yet be. It is not easy to forget those experiences, neither for the ethnographer nor for the Jugoslavs. Only in the most recent years has that ultimate symbol of identity, language, begun to shift its prestige to the urban mode; until now, it has been the dialect of the peasant, like that of the Bedouin, that has commanded respect (Magner 1967; Nader 1962).

Thus it is that the attitudes toward the peasant in Jugoslavia (and in the Balkans in general) are maddening in their inconsistency. In a world which is modern, he is despised for his conservatism, in a world of cosmopolitan yearnings for his parochial outlook, in a Communist milieu for bearing the seed of capitalism, while he is the seed of the nation. Jugoslavia again finds itself in the nutcracker; how can one damn the idiocy of rural life when that life is the cradle of national consciousness? How can one cherish local tradition when that tradition has set Serb against Croat, Orthodox against Moslem for centuries? How, indeed, can one regard peasant life as a positive moral force in nation-building when the consciousness of Slavic unity came first from men named Herder and Goethe?

For most Jugoslavs, these philosophical questions are remote. More central is the conflict between tradition and modernity, between the security of belonging to the closed society of the village and the lure of mobility in the urban world. Across all this lies the network of kinship, binding in its loyalties, yet permissive in its expansion. Jugoslavia is a small country, so that no matter where a man goes, it is only a day or two from where he has been, even by the most humble transportation. The changes in urban culture are rapidly transmitted to the village, in knowledge if not in fact, so that industrialization does not split the country as it might. Visits between peasant families and those of their members who have gone off to the town or city are quite frequent. Towns and cities are invariably administrative centers for the surrounding countryside, and peasants always have some business to conduct in them. When they come to town, they usually stay with their sons or brothers or cousins. Town dwellers frequently visit the old homestead; if the father of the family is still alive and on the farm, his sons, with their families, frequently return to celebrate the yearly *slava*. On these occasions goods and information are invariably exchanged. When a son comes home to visit, he brings some money to contribute to the expenses of the farm; often, sons continue to send part of their wages home to their parents. He may bring useful items that are easier to obtain in the larger towns—a good jackknife, a food grinder, some rubber boots. Daughters and wives will bring a bit of knitting, or embroidery, but most often some kind of food, like jams or candies. When the peasants come to town, it is with baskets full of their cheeses, fresh fruit, a suckling pig tied by a string to its hind leg, and demijohns of brandy or wine. Sons and sons-in-law will give advice on how to handle the bureaucracy, daughters will help their mothers shop, and children will initiate their country cousins into the wonders of the city. Inevitably, everyone ends up at the cinema. The agnatic web is strong, and if there have been changes in the kinship system, they have been not so much in the weakening of kinship as in the use of different kinds of links—affinal, uterine, ritual—to a greater degree than was the case in the village.

Inevitably, as the family shifts to the city, the center of the network also shifts. Successful sons, after their father's death, assume his role as head of the network in an urban locus. Brothers living in towns then tend to visit brothers in cities, and there is still a good deal of mutual help, in the exchange of money and advice, in boarding nephews so that they can go to the university or a technical school, and so on. But even when all the relatives are gone from the country, urbanites still visit there. The more affluent buy summer houses an easy drive from town, and those with discriminating palates go regularly to get their favorite wine, or brandy, the best cheese and smoked ham. These purchases are not made in the marketplace so much as they are through personal contacts. One does not go to Bjelo Polje, as a village, to buy a demijohn of brandy; one goes to visit old "Uncle" Mark, who has been saving it since last winter for just this buyer. And when Uncle Mark comes to Belgrade to buy his wife a sewing machine, he brings a bottle with him, perhaps as a gift, and he may stay the night, and surely he will be guided to the store that this week has the best machines at the best price. If he wants a new radio, the electrician on the third floor will be called in for advice—what make, what store, which clerk to ask for, and say that Milan sent you. Not too many months later, the electrician will be getting his brandy from Uncle Mark. There are no impersonal catalogs, no Consumer Reports, no Good Housekeeping Seals—just people. This is a society that has been turned upside down by a ravaging war, a bloody revolution, a process of industrialization that has compressed the experience of the United States into a generation, but almost nothing happens on an impersonal basis. Even city dwellers are not liberated from particularism; although the lure of the new supermarkets is strong, the best meat comes from the butcher your mother used to buy from, the best tomatoes from that old woman in the corner of the piazza.

Much of this personalism stems from the fact that the mobility of individuals, however great, has been carried out in a small geographical compass. It is not just that Jugoslavia is a small country, but that Serbian sons who leave the farm seldom go outside of Serbia. Slovenians stay in Slovenia, or at most go to Croatia. There are exceptions, of course; the higher one goes in the occupational scale, the more frequently one encounters persons who come from greater distances. Since it is no more difficult, in the physical sense, for a man from Maribor to take a job in Belgrade than it is for a man from Nis, the limitations must be social ones. Language is among the first of these; Slovenians find it hard going in Serbia, as do Macedonians, since these two languages and Serbian are not mutually intelligible. On the other hand, there are no real barriers to communication between Bosnians and Serbs, Montenegrins and Croats, as far as language is concerned. The real barriers lie in a sense of identity and group membership that is epitomized in the reliance on kinship and friendship networks. In a society which only a few years ago consisted of small villages with only a nascent national elite, and which only a generation before that consisted of pioneer families pushing into a wilderness (in Serbia), it is small wonder that one trusts the people one knows, and few others. In a society that has known severe religious divisions and a succession of foreign ideologies (including the last one), it is hard to put one's faith in the abstract, on a national level.

The Balkan peasant, at least in the Jugoslav example, is thus in a position today which has changed its specific form but not its style. He still lives in the shadow of competing giants, taking some things, recombining others to make a unique blend. He still lives surrounded by people more than by things or rules or organizations. The agnatic core that was important to the Slav in fording the Danube a millenium and a half ago, to the Montenegrin in ordering his political life, to the Serb in retaking his lands from the

Turk, is important today in finding a job, in sending a son to school, in getting a pig for the holidays. It is particularly important in the movement of a farm family into the urban sphere, just as it was important a hundred years ago in moving from the mountains into the plains. Typically, it is the sons who go out into the industrial world, or perhaps only the youngest and best educated. His base is firm—food can always be sent; if he is lonely and confused, he can visit; if he fails, he can come home. When his new position is established, another brother comes to stay and go to high school, a second gets a job through personal influence; but they go back home for the *slava*. When the immigrant marries and (often as not) puts his wife to work, the mother comes to cook and clean, and perhaps to raise the children. Joint families do not form, nor do agnatic clusters, for housing is too scarce to allow such choices, but when newcomers build their own houses, as they do in many provincial towns, agnates build near one another.

The viability of the family core is impressive. Rather than being weakened by the growth of mining and industry in rural areas, it was strengthened when sons so employed were able to contribute cash to meet family needs. Rather than being destroyed by the upheavals and rapid mobility of industrialization, it has served as the orienting thread and conduit of mobility. Now, there is always some question as to whether an industrial society can function when particularism is that entrenched. Our model of industrial society is one in which universalistic procedures apply, and in which recruitment is open to all on the basis of qualification. But we confuse our democratic rhetoric with reality and forget that American mobility was based on enormous transferrals of populations in an age of primitive communication when moving meant leaving the group as well as the locale. Kinship-oriented particularism was minimal, not because it was dysfunctional but because it was impossible. In the first place, there is no reason why particularistic recruitment rules cannot place qualified people into empty statuses. Particularistic recruitment seems to work very well in academia and among plumbers, for example. Rarely will the requirements of a job be so strict and the population from which recruits come so small, that the system would suffer from a bit of nepotism. After all, one man's nephew is as good as another's. More important than any theoretical, systematic notions of how an industrial society should work is the question of how it must work when people move into a strange cultural environment. It need not be far away from home, but the world of machines, of train schedules, of time clocks to be punched, of sustained effort for eight hours, is a new and different world. A man cannot enter that world without someone to trust as a guide. Who better than his uncle? He will learn faster, agreements will be kept more frequently, more work will be done. Not only will the new worker trust his uncle, but the boss will trust him because he knows his uncle. If we are sufficiently objective to judge a system by its results, a look at Japan, or at family firms in East Africa, or even at the progress of immigrants in large cities in the United States should convince us. Some day, the Balkan peasant may change, just as many Americans have changed. But for the moment he lives in the same world of people that wet their feet in the Danube to face the Roman legions.*

* The author is indebted to Prof. Charles Jelavich for his comments on this paper but of course remains responsible for the historical ambiguities which must remain in so discursive a treatment.

ALEX WEINGROD

Cultural Traditions in Developing Societies: Great, Little & Mass

Writing in the 1920's, Ortega y Gasset cast an anguished eye at his native Spain and, more generally, at Europe. "There is one fact," he wrote, "which whether for good or ill is of utmost importance in the public life of Europe at the present moment. This fact is the accession of the masses to complete social power . . . It is called the rebellion of the masses." (Ortega y Gasset 1932). To Ortega, this rebellion was "for ill" and not "for good": mass society and mass culture spelled the doom of civilization, an end to "high culture," and the crowning of mediocrity and vulgarity. It was democracy and equality run amok—the end of the social, political and economic order that had brought such brilliance to Europe.

Mass society and mass culture have, of course, been topics of much scholarly interest and controversy. De Tocqueville, who seems to have said everything worth saying, long ago commented upon the emerging democratic American Man. In more recent years, from Dwight MacDonald to T. S. Eliot and from C. Wright Mills to Edward Shils, sociologists, historians, and literary critics have argued the merits and failures of contemporary mass man and mass culture.

Curiously, however, this debate has not moved far outside of the Western world. When we study American or French culture

and society we write about "elites," "consumers," "taste manu-
facturers," "hipsters," and "hippies." Yet when we write about
Indian or Middle Eastern culture and society we write about
"great and little tradition," "urban and rural," "peasant and
townsman." In the face of all the evidence of massive changes that
have transformed the developing states, our major categories of
cultural analysis have a quaint ring to them (Friedl 1964:569-587).

Let me be a bit more specific. There is growing evidence of a
shrinking of social and cultural distance between city and countryside throughout the developing world. Such processes as migration,
a spreading urbanization, the market orientation of the countryside, the new networks of transportation and the new media, have
all contributed to narrowing the distance between city and village.
As the social and cultural gaps become narrowed, the anthropologist's analytic categories also need to be revised. If, for example,
"great and little" tradition is appropriate conceptually to "traditional" India, then (for want of a better term) a "national" tradition may be a better concept to characterize "modernizing" India.
Similarly, if "rural" and "urban" were appropriate analytic categories to the Mexico of thirty years ago, then "provincial" and
"metropolitan" may be better terms for contemporary Mexico.
More generally, it seems likely that "class" and "locality" are no
longer accurate predictors of "culture," and that to an ever-increas-
ing degree the more meaningful cultural distinctions are between
generations. It is to processes such as these that we refer when we
speak of "mass society" and "mass culture." I would argue that
these concepts are pertinent to the south of India as well as to the
American South, and to a village in Ghana as much as to a village
in the Vaucluse.

Before proceeding further it is necessary to get a clearer idea of
what terms such as "national tradition" or "metropolitan and provincial" mean. National tradition refers to the prominence given
to national personalities and issues in modern and modernizing
societies. The national rather than the local or regional arena is
emphasized, and a variety of political leaders, entertainers, poets
and even scientists may play roles on that stage. The national tradi-

tion is secular, and it depends upon good mass-communications and a wide-ranging audience. In this regard the national tradition is similar to the "popular culture" which also emphasizes personalities and depends upon mass-communications.

As the national (and also the popular) tradition grows in force and in scope, the cultural distinctions between city and countryside become less pronounced. The same styles are followed in village and city, the same consumer goods are desired and acquired, the same magazines are read and radios listened to. Thus city and countryside are not different types, but rather represent different points on a single cultural continuum. "Metropolitan" refers to the active edge of the continuum—the place where the styles are set and the fashions dictated. The "provincial" zones follow the lead of the metropolitan center. The point to be emphasized is that these are not different ways or styles of living, but rather the more or less successful expressions of the same customs and cultural ideals.

In this section I would like to further outline these distinctions by referring briefly to two rapidly changing societies: Israel and Sardinia. These two are especially useful illustrations of changing cultural traditions since they are at different points in the process of modernization. Both Israel and Sardinia are, of course, culturally Western, and I will follow this brief review with an equally brief examination of a contemporary non-Western society.

For the purposes of this article Israel exemplifies three general points: political nationalism, an emphasis upon the national arena, and a fading away of rural-urban distinctions. These developments are well advanced in Israel, and they are also pertinent to the transformations now taking place throughout the world.

That Zionism, or political nationalism, has been a major emphasis in Israeli society and culture needs little amplification. Since the earliest days of Jewish colonization Zionism has been, to use Apter's term, a kind of "political religion": the nation and the nation's leaders have been a primary focus of loyalty and solidarity.

To be sure, various other loyalties—religious, ethnic, or class—have also been powerful. Yet the nation, its symbols and its heroes, has loomed large in the public and private consciousness.

In Israel various national-level political, economic and social organizations have taken precedence over local-level organization. It is not hard to see why this should be the case. The country and its population are comparatively small, and taken together with the socialist-planning policies of its leadership, this has meant that authority in many spheres has become centralized. In a country so small it may be possible, if frequently clumsy, to direct affairs from the center. Equally important, the crucial issues that have faced the populace have been national issues—questions of war and peace, devaluation, immigration, development and welfare economics.

Given these circumstances it is not surprising to find that cultural distinctions between city, town or village are frequently blurred. The society is small in size and number; transportation is excellent; the media of radio, film and now television are widely diffused. In addition, informal communications networks crisscross the entire society; there are a series of regular circumstances under which persons from widely separate locales come into contact. Moreover, many of the communities in the hinterland have insisted upon maintaining an urban life-style. A *kibbutz* in the north boasts a museum, a town of sixty thousand establishes a junior college, a *moshav* in the south is regularly visited by a company of actors. Thus the styles of life in city and countryside do not differ in content—there is no cultural split between rural and urban. This is not to say, of course, that there are no cultural differences between a Tel Aviv, a Beersheba, and a *kibbutz*. It is rather to urge that the difference is better seen as one between metropolitan and provincial rather than rural and urban. Tel Aviv is more sophisticated, more varied, and more style conscious; but these are differences in degree, not in kind.

What the Israeli case represents, then, is the accentuation of national society and national traditions. Since it is an egalitarian society there is no proper aristocracy; there are, instead, a variety of elites. The elites, who are style setters, include army heroes, soccer players, stage personalities, successful businessmen, and so forth. Since the society is so compact in scale, and since the mass media are well developed, cultural innovations are quickly communicated across the entire social system; for example, the same joke or bit of juicy gossip will be known immediately to a diverse range of persons spread over a large area.

Although no society is ever typical, Israeli society is much too atypical to make it easily comparable to other modernizing situations. Sardinia, on the other hand, is an example with better promise of comparability; it is an economically poor zone, a land dotted with old villages and market towns, a once feudal area with a heritage that is now bent upon development. What does the Sardinian case show?

It is perhaps better to begin by indicating what the Sardinian case fails to show. One searches in vain in Sardinia for a gentry, an aristocracy of breeding and taste, for cultural brokers or for village little traditions. They are just not to be found. There are, indeed, no peasants, but rather "post-peasants." As we have been told in many novels and numerous films, the old landed aristocrats have retreated into their museum-like homes, while their offspring are tuned-in to fast cars, tennis, and the jet-set. There is no class or category of persons who mediate culturally between city and countryside: those who still live in the villages or small towns receive their cultural cues from television, the fashion magazines, trips to the city or to Rome, or from the many Sards who have recently left the island to work in Turin or Germany. In Sardinia, tourism also informs the popular tastes: the Costa Smerelda, with its yachts filled with the "beautiful people," has a powerful cultural impact upon mountain villages as well as the city bourgeoisie.

In Sardinia, then, the gap between city and countryside has been narrowed. The villager who takes the bus to shop in town is not confused or in awe: he has seen the mass-consumer goods advertised on television, or a migrant cousin or brother may have taught him to prefer a French to an Italian product. Moreover, the towns and cities are themselves bulging with other villagers who have migrated during the past twenty years: many of the city dwellers are at most a generation away from the village, and chains of village-city contact produce a regular flow of awareness. Thus, in Sardinia as in Israel, the distinction is not between rural and urban, but rather between provincial and metropolitan. Taking a wider focus one can also see how Sardinia as a whole is "provincial" in relation to a "metropolitan" Rome. Indeed, the Sards themselves are all too aware of the provincial character of their island—the fashions to be followed, the tastes that are set, are stamped in Rome rather than in Cagliari.

The "national tradition" in Sardinia is not nationalistic—there is no Sard equivalent of Zionism. The Sards are much too shrewd and cynical to accept another nationalism. Rather, theirs is a "popular culture," with its emphasis upon consumption and consumer heroes—soccer teams and players, movie stars, the fabulously successful businessmen of the North, rock-and-roll combos. In conversation, in view on the screen or reported on the radio, in dozens of magazines, these are major cultural leaders and issues. Cultural organization in Sardinia is best thought of as mass culture with competing elites, and cultural modes followed irrespective of social class or locality.

While it is correct, I think, to urge that city and countryside have grown closer to one another, it is also important to take note of a different cultural distinction: namely, the cultural distinctions that separate generations. This is not a simple matter to characterize; every generation, after all, sees the next as following different cultural modes, less traditional in practice, radical or even nihilistic in outlook. Yet there do appear to be special features to the contemporary differences between generations. Since Sardinia has changed greatly in the past twenty years it is reasonable to assume that young people diverge more and more from their elders. Parents remember Fascism, some with nostalgia, others with distaste; the young are typically bored with politics. Parents recall economic scarcity; the young have seen department stores and supermarkets, and they are accustomed, at least in principle, to the idea of plenty. Technological changes—the mass media, the pill, migration and travel, new industrial skills—are an acceptable part of a young person's cultural inventory. Equally important, a kind of "youth culture" is emphasized in the new consumer society: the wonderful ways of the young are celebrated in the movies, on television, in hit songs, in advertisements. Not everyone will drive a sleek car or leave the village for the romance of Rome: yet the young person who buys the hit records or the young girl who makes a modish dress, is able to keep touch with what is modern. As youth culture grows in Sardinia, it is reasonable to speculate that some young people will have more in common with their peers in Rome and Milan—and, by extension, Paris, London and beyond—than with their own family and their own locale. In brief, while one set of cultural distinctions has diminished, a second becomes increasingly significant.

Several years ago Clifford Geertz wrote that "most of the rural people commonly referred to as peasants in Western Europe, Japan and much of Latin America stand in complementary relationship not to a classical great tradition, a bazaar-type market system, or a traditional hereditary elite, but to modern mass culture, highly-industrialized economy, and a thoroughly bureaucratized government." (Geertz 1962:2). Sardinia and Israel may fit this type; but what of the non-Western nations? How should the cultural traditions of the post-colonial world be characterized?

India is perhaps the best place to pursue these questions. There is already a mountainous Indian literature, ranging from the intellectual's introspections regarding "continuity and change" to an impressive number of village studies, and including as well excellent research into national politics and mass communications. What do these studies have to say regarding national and popular culture, city and countryside, youth culture and mass society?

In village-level research as well as in studies of cultural process the anthropologist's emphasis has typically been upon the continuity, if in new wrappings, of the Hindu Great Tradition. This view is well expressed in Milton Singer's studies of cultural organization in Madras (Singer 1959). Singer shows that although new media such as films may be used, the themes of the film are based in traditional Hindu lore. Essentially, this is a case of "old wine in new bottles"—the medium is *not* the message. Singer's point is that while there may be a variety of new cultural performances, the themes are the classic ones, and the audience is composed of the same kinds of persons who for generations have witnessed analogous performances. In much the same vein many of the village studies also report upon a continuity in ritual, in caste relationships, and more generally in the isolation of the countryside. Illiteracy is widespread, the mass media are not widely diffused, and village society is surely a long way from being "consumer oriented."

While there clearly is a still-evolving classic tradition, there is also evidence of a rapidly emerging kind of national tradition. Not all Indian films, after all, deal with the classical themes; in the mass-circulation magazines and newspapers political personalities, film stars and sports heros are celebrated (cf. Barnouw and Krishnaswamy 1963). It even seems likely that, if one were to listen long enough to the radio, one might hear the Beatles or their Indian counterparts. Different cultural styles compete in the urban centers, and modernity also percolates into the countryside. Side by side with the classic tradition one also sees signs of a national, and perhaps also, a popular culture.

The evidence of a national tradition is best exemplified in studies of Indian politics. The struggle for Indian independence, the Indian nationalist movements, brought new styles and new personalities to the consciousness of all Indians. While the more recent national leadership does not reach such heroic proportions, the major parties are mass parties and thus provide a whole array of new social settings. Myron Weiner, the political scientist, has shown how the political parties become an important focus of solidarity in the cities (Weiner 1957). Kathleen Gough's work in Kerala (Gough 1965:363-372), and Adrian Mayer's studies of an Indian town (Mayer 1966:97-121), make much the same point. In an interesting article entitled "India's Two Political Cultures," Weiner describes the contrasts between the parochial local politicians and the London School of Economics-trained Delhi intellectuals: while the "two cultures" diverge in content and in style, the need for communication and cooperation between them gives life to an expanding national political arena (Weiner 1964). In brief, in the Indian case as elsewhere, political organization reaches throughout the society to promote new loyalities, new outlooks and new behavior.

Do the same life-styles encompass city and village in India? Although the gap continues to be very wide, there is evidence that as transportation and communication links are perfected, as migration to the cities increases, and as national organizational links are forged, city and countryside do grow closer. F. G. Bailey's study of two villages in Orissa is an excellent case in point: Bisipara, a remote village, surely appears to be "rural;" on the other hand, Cutack, adjacent to a market town, may be better thought of as "provincial" (Bailey 1963). In Bisipara one dresses differently than do the townsfolk, and participates in local ritual; at Cutack, one dresses as a townsman, but there is no place to go. There must be a great many rural villages similar to Bisipara—but it is likely that many more become like Cutack. Provincialism is spreading in contemporary India.

What of "youth culture"? Generation differences are certainly profound; yet it is doubtful that youth culture can be said to exist outside the privilegd circle of urban middle- and upper-class families. The "Mersey beat" is not yet heard throughout the subcontinent. One supposes, though, that if and when Indian society becomes more urbanized and industrialized, the cultural distinctions between generations will also become more significant.

In brief conclusion let me make clear that to say that cultural processes in an India or an Egypt can be usefully analyzed in terms of mass society and mass culture is not to say that this process is identical with "Westernization." As the Japanese have so clearly shown, mass culture is not specifically Western. Rather, a "national" culture in India is tuned-in to Indian history and tradition, and no matter how much Coca-Cola is consumed in the Middle East, Cairo does not become New York. To be sure, cultural developments in future years are certain to follow strange and unknown channels—yet whatever the influences and hybrids, the products are unlikely to be uniformly Western. To quote T. S. Eliot: "Every change we make is tending to bring about a new civilization of the nature of which we are ignorant." Eliot finished by adding, "and in which we should all of us be unhappy" (Eliot 1949:16). Whether or not Eliot's pessimism regarding mass culture is correct, surely it is a theme that needs further investigation.

EVA HUNT & ROBERT HUNT

The Role of Courts in Rural Mexico

INTRODUCTION

More than a decade ago, Wolf (1956), following a general suggestion of Steward (1950), pointed out that Mesoamerican studies were in need of refocusing. He indicated that we had to move from the intensive study of isolated communities to an understanding of how local, small social aggregates interlocked with larger sociopolitical units, including nation-oriented groups. One part of the new type of studies involved the study of cultural brokers, "nation-oriented individuals from local communities who have established ties with the national level." The importance of the brokers was that they stood ". . . guard over crucial junctures or synapses of relationships which connect the local system to the larger whole" (Wolf 1956:1075).

This paper is one of several dealing with these problems (cf. Hunt and Hunt 1967; R. Hunt 1968). More specifically, we are concerned with symbiotic relations between communities within a politically and socioculturally defined region. Following Wolf's general suggestions, we conducted fieldwork in a district in the north of the state of Oaxaca, Mexico. Although we worked most intensively in a few specific communities, we focused our research on the whole area, specifically on the interlocking of units in the local-regional system, and on the ties of the region as a whole with

the larger sociopolitical units of the state. In a multiple society like
Mexico (cf. Nash 1957), where more than one social segment and
culture shares the definition and boundaries of the society, and
where contact between segments tends to be impersonal, formal,
and even antagonistic, there is a group of institutions which carries
the main burden of communication between segments (R. Hunt
1968). Although individuals in isolation may play the role of brokers, many brokers are actually agents of what we call interface institutions. We prefer to make the distinction between institutional
and individual contexts, thereby allowing the inclusion of formal
and informal broker roles, as well as impersonal institutions, like
the marketplace, which may function independently of personal-
ized agents.

We focus on the court because it offers several strategic advan-
tages from the point of view of our interests. First, the court is a
formalized institution, and, in a country like Mexico, one with extensive written records on "double institutionalized norms" (Bohannan 1965:33-42). The national law can be compared and
contrasted with local customary law, as well as with norms of other
kinds at the community level. Understanding its functions at different levels of integration allows us to contrast and compare the
juridical aspects of the cultures represented in the multiple society.
Since officers in a Mexican court deal with cases coming from all
segments of the society, they occupy the role of broker, and the
court functions as an interface institution. We hope that this description will contribute to the general undeerstanding of how an
Indian peasantry living in closed or semi-closed corporate communities, a rural class of nation-oriented Mestizos, and the other segments of Mexican society interact at the local levels, within a
region, and through the court.

The paper, however, makes another point. Laura Nader (1966:
382) has pointed out that there is a scarcity of comparative data
and analyses on the functioning of the court in Mexico. She has
already published some pioneering articles dealing with the courts
at the municipal level (i.e., the community level) in two Zapotecan

towns (Nader 1964a, 1964b, 1965, 1966; cf. also Nader and Metz-ger 1963; Metzger 1960; Black and Metzger 1965). We use a differ-ent set of axes: one is the inter-locking of the municipal and district court systems; the other is the function of the district court as an integrative but primarily conservative institution.

THE POPULATION

In the area of Mexico which we discuss, the district we call San Juan, the two most noticeable sociocultural segments are Indians, who speak three distinct Indian languages, and rural Mexicans or Mestizos, speakers of Spanish. Besides language, a number of significant cultural and social-organization differences exist be-tween the two segments. Communities in this area can easily be distinguished as belonging to one or another segment, in spite of degrees of acculturation; language is a reliable indicator because the communties cluster at both ends of a continuum with a marked gap in between, both with regard to language and other traits (see Figure 1).

Figure I. Distribution of Communities in the San Juan District by Lan-guage and Number of Cases Brought to the District Court

Number of Municipios	Number of Settlement Communities	Popula-tion	% of Speakers of an Indian Language	No. of Cases Brought to the San Juan Court	No. of Cases per 1000 Inhabi-tants	Group Definition Indian	Mestizo
3	4	3431	100%	22	6.42	I	
6	8	8306	95-99%	65	7.82	II	
4	12	9639	91-94%	87	9.02	III	
1	3	1428	80%	36	25.21	IV	
2	5	6141	62-70%	74	12.05	V	
3	16	9998	0-10%	113	11.3		VI

For some purposes of analysis, these communities can be put on a continuum between two cultural poles, Indian and Mestizo. Communities in the San Juan district, however, tend to cluster at the opposite ends. Groups I and II are highly conservative, traditional, closed corporate villages. Group III includes traditional communities which, in spite of their "corporateness," have maintained, for historical reasons (e.g., they were capitals of pre-Hispanic chiefdoms), sporadic but open communication with the outside world. Group IV, a single *municipio,* is a single community with two outlying hamlet-settlements, internally and externally defined as corporate Indian, but with a high degree of unrest and disorganization brought about by several factors, both internal (e.g., conflict over water for irrigation) and external (e.g., loss of land through recent expropriation). The degree of internal anarchy is reflected in the number of cases brought to court. Group V includes open Indian communities which are more acculturated and in which a minority class of the local population identifies itself as Mestizo oriented. Group VI is composed of three macro-*municipios,* located in the major valley in the district, the population of which has considered itself Mexican since at least the end of the eighteenth century. A minority of Indian speakers (less than 10%), incorporated into the local lower class, is not made up of locally born Indians but of recent immigrants from the mountain communities which make up the Indian hinterland of the district. For the purposes of this paper, Groups I to V are considered Indian; Group VI is Mestizo-Mexican.

The Two Types of Courts

The district court, *Juzgado de Primera Instancia,* is located in the *cabecera* or capital of the district of San Juan. This town is also the *cabecera* of the largest, most densely populated *municipio* of the district and, as could be expected, it is a Mexican-Mestizo community. The town of San Juan itself has approximately 2000 inhabitants, and even before the Conquest it dominated the region, since it had been the capital of the major pre-Hispanic state.

The district court is located in a separate building in the town square, facing the local government offices and market and adjacent to the jail. The judge and the two other officers of the district court are appointed civil servants, representatives of the national urban segment of the nation with its paraphernalia of bureaucratic procedures, its different ideals and goals, and its overwhelming political and economic power. [All major authors dealing with the problem of the distribution of political and economic power in Mexico agree on this last point (cf. Aguirre Beltran 1967; Brandenburg 1964; Gonzales 1965; Padgett 1966; and Scott 1964).] At the time of our study none of the official appointees was locally born.

The officers of the municipal community courts, however, are local citizens, officers elected by their communities for short periods of tenure, and selected as representatives according to traditional, local procedures (the civil-religious hierarchy which characterizes Indian communities in Mexico). The municipal courts do not have separate buildings; their affairs are transacted in the local government offices (the *Ayuntamiento* or *Cabildo*).

The district court functions both as a civil and a criminal court. It is run by a lawyer appointed by the Mexican bureaucracy as judge (*Juez*), and his term of office is decided from above in terms of his qualifications. Below him work two other court officers: a secretary (*Secretario*) who takes responsibility in the judge's absence, deals with the preliminaries of cases, and is, in general, second in command. The second official is an *Ejecutor,* combining the roles of executor, treasurer and scribe. His major function is recording cases and notifying the persons involved in them. The qualification for these posts is experience, not a professional degree.

The judge also oversees the local jail, which is guarded by a "keeper of the keys" (*Alcalde de Cárceles*) and several municipal policemen (the court does not have its own police). To economize on personnel, the judge is also the appointed head of the District Civil Register with its assistant scribe (*Escribiente*). These official distinctions of role may be blurred in practice. Although the judge makes the final decision in all cases, minor cases may be decided by the *Secretario,* and in the absence of these officers (or when they are too busy elsewhere) the court scribe may deal with them. The picture is even more complicated because the formally separate office of the *Ministerio Público* may take on some of the functions of the court. The post of *Agente del Ministerio Público* is the district bureaucratic equivalent of the state attorney general: it combines the roles of coroner, detective in charge of investigating cases for the state (or by petition of the judge or plaintiff), and prosecutor. In San Juan however, the *agente* may deal directly with cases without the judge's supervision. This informal arrangement varies from one district to another, as well as within a court, depending on the personal amity and trust between the individuals occupying the respective posts. Informal, extrabureaucratic arrangements are not unique to San Juan. Blau (1955), in dealing with agencies in the U.S., has shown how considerations of a personal nature, or the interaction patterns of officers in a bureaucratic agency, may create an informal decision-making network which is different from official policy.

At the municipal level, three officers of the *municipio* are theoretically in charge of the court: the *Presidente,* the *Cíndico,* and the *Alcalde Constitucional* or *Regidor.* The last post receives the title of judge locally. The *Cíndico* is the municipal, *pro forma* equivalent of the *Ministerio Público.* In the *municipio* of San Andres, however, the *Presidente* is in charge of most decisions assisted by the whole of the municipal body, including all officers. The other roles, however, do not function as expected by formal definition. In cases of doubt, expert witnesses among the elders of the community are brought in as participants in the process of decision making, primarily to mitigate individual responsibility for the final outcome, and to avoid personal vendettas. In some cases involving an individual defendant versus the municipio (as plaintiff), the court is superseded by a town meeting in which all the household heads participate.

There is probably a high degree of local variation in the procedures of municipal courts. San Andres stands in an intermediate position when compared with Nader's Talea or Juquila (i.e., it fits neither pattern exactly, although it approximates that of Juquila). Since we did not study other municipal courts with the same degree of intensity as San Andres, controlled internal comparisons within our district are not possible. But our general knowledge of the functioning of other municipal courts suggests that the degree of variation is very high.

The district court keeps a bureaucratic schedule, approximately from 10 A.M. to 4:30 P.M., closing for lunch. In contrast, the municipal courts adjust their time schedules to the demands of the local population. They hear cases around 5 to 6 A.M., before the peasant goes to work in his fields, or at sunset, after he has returned from work. Occasionally, females (who stay in town) may bring cases at other hours during the day, but all cases in which witnesses are required and at which final decisions are made are tried at hours which are convenient for the clients of the court. In fact, the court officers themselves may be engaged during daylight hours in their own agricultural work. Indians often complain that the office hours of the district court are highly inconvenient. In most cases, this schedule forces the Indian to stay away from his village overnight in San Juan, and to incur extra expenditures of scarce cash. Because of this, many cases unsatisfactorily solved at the municipal level are never taken to the district court.

The district court serves a population of approximately 40,000 inhabitants in 19 *municipios,* which range in population from 927 to 5,882. The district and municipal boundaries are determined by the state government. These boundaries tend to coincide with traditional *provincias* and with the Porfirian political units (ex-*Distritos*). Today, though they tend to overlap state, congressional or electoral districts, these are not always identical. Both municipal and district boundaries can change independently through time. Thus, in the history of San Juan, municipal fission from the court district has not been uncommon.

When the population of a *municipio* becomes highly dissatisfied with the functioning of its district court, they may send their cases to the court of an adjacent district. During the period of our sample, three communities outside the district brought cases to San Juan, which was jurisdictionally irregular. In the same period, at least two communities in the San Juan district took cases to a territorially adjacent district court.

THE EVIDENCE

Our data are in several forms. We have extensive interviews with court officers and with local citizens who have had contact with legal procedures and the courts. We observed activities in both kinds of courts, district and municipal. Approximately two months of the period of fieldwork in San Juan were dedicated primarily to work on the district court. In San Andres, the Indian *municipio*, court observation was not so systematic, taking place sporadically during the regular field season.

We also have information in our notes on 572 cases on record in San Juan and San Andres during the period from 1958 to 1963. Five hundred and four are from the district court in San Juan. Of these, 493 originated in settlements within the legal boundaries of the district, and 11 came from towns outside the district. For the Indian *municipio* we have 68 cases. Although it has been stated that some municipal courts do not keep records, in San Andres there has been a tradition of careful record-keeping for at least 20 years, supported by the presence of a typewriter and a literate municipal officer who rejoices in the task.

In the course of analysing our data, we have quite explicitly adopted a somewhat unusual research strategy. Our data are of two sorts. The largest proportion comes from participant observation and from formal and informal interviews. This was not guided by any particular set of hypotheses, but was systematized to cover information on areas we thought or suspected might be significant (e.g., how does the judge treat witchcraft cases?). Secondly, we have the court cases which we have culled from court archives and checked with informants. From these data we have generated patterns of action to define the courts' structures and functions. We have then generated statistically testable hypotheses about the distributions of court cases which would serve to confirm or deny pattern statements. We have therefore generated statements about culture pattern, like most anthropologists, but we have attempted to support our pattern statement with statistical procedures.

In the statistical treatment of the district court cases on record, we have removed the 11 cases from outside the district. We decided on the basis of inspection that their exclusion did not significantly change the statistical results. Since they are anomalous—in the sense of being from towns of which we have no personal knowledge, and of radically skewing the data with respect to number of cases per 1000 population—we omitted them from our statistical tabulation. The municipal court of San Andres serves a population of 2175, of which 978 are located in the *cabecera,* and the remaining 1197 in 5 subordinate settlements. The sixty-eight cases primarily represent the *cabecera* itself. The subordinate political units handle many minor local cases themselves, at the submunicipal level, which are not recorded in, and are not taken to, the *cabecera.* They are often handled in the hamlet itself, outside of a legal context.

The district court is located in the town of San Juan, and thus serves a double function. Although San Juan has a municipal governing body, the presence of the district court siphons local cases directly to it. We have clear evidence that the distribution of cases sent to the district court is not similar to the distribution of cases heard at the local municipal level, and that these differences are highly significant for the structure of the district, statistically.

To preserve all the cases from the town of San Juan would produce a biassing effect by artificially increasing the percentage and distributions of all Mestizo cases brought to the district court, when comparing different ethnic segments. To correct for this effect, when it comes to assessing the contribution of the district capital to the total of cases in the district, we derived a method for statistically removing from the San Juan collection those cases which could be assigned to the local function of the court, and retained only those which could be assigned to the district function. In order to do this, we calculated the number of cases per 1000 inhabitants of each type which all the towns in the *municipio* of San Juan (minus San Juan itself) brought to court. The population of San Juan was then multiplied by these proportions, and an estimate of San Juan's contribution to the district court was thereby produced. These estimates were then added to the tabulations for the rest of the *municipio*. The totals are treated as the contribution of their whole *municipio* of San Juan to the district court. This reduces the undesirable weight of the *cabecera* cases in the total computations. This reduction, in theory, works against supporting our hypothesis.

After extensive ethnographic probing, cases have been grouped in the charts by what we have considered to be significant cultural categories for both Indians and Mestizos. These comprise groupings which are not identical with legal definitions according to the Mexican codes. It is necessary, therefore, to indicate the contents of the groupings for those interested in comparisons. Murder or homicide includes the same cases as the Mexican legal code: attempts to take a person's (not oneself's) life which end directly or indirectly in the decease of the victim. The Mexican code defines it originally as "depriving a person of his life" (Código Penal:1964: 93). Cases of attempted homicide not ending in death are classified as injuries.

Injuries include a variety of physical attacks on persons resulting in physical markings, grave or minor wounds, excoriations, fractures, burns, etc. It excludes, however, simple beatings, slaps, and other minor forms of physical aggression. This category is also identical with the Mexican legal code. Other cases Against Persons is a residual category combining several categories otherwise distinct in Mexican law; it excludes crimes against (or caused by) public officers and the state, as well as matters pertaining to family honor (see definition below). Thus, this varied category includes threats (including threats of witchcraft), beatings, insults, libel and slander, breach of confidence in business or intimate matters, and simple assault.

The category of Property includes cases of conflict over inheritance, theft, breaking and entering, rustling, invasion of public property (such as entering the communal pastures of a town without permission), damage to private property (arson, and willful destruction of objects, plants or animals not owned by the person committing the act), fraud involving property, despoiling, and falsification of property titles of real estate. The category of cases dealing with the honor or stability of the Family includes most (but not all) of several distinct categories on the Mexican criminal and civil codes. Some of the categories of the Mexican criminal code dealing with this group are sexual offenses, offenses against an individual's (rather than a family's) honor, and offenses against public morals. For our typology, this group includes cases of rape, elopement, attempted rape or elopement, seduction of minors, abandonment of a dependent kinsman of spouse (elder parent, child, other dependent collateral minors), divorce, separation, adultery and kidnapping. Both Mestizos and Indians group all these actions as pertaining directly to the family, and as being threats against the family as a group rather than against individuals. In this classification we have followed our informants' views, not only because of their psychological reality, but because in terms of the social structure they are treated (and affect action) in a similar manner.

Crimes against Constituted Authority includes all those cases dealing with relations between government officers and individuals or groups of citizens in their respective capacities. Thus, it involves officials as either defendant or plaintiff, and comprises cases which Mexican law treats as crimes against the state, disobedience of authority, and offenses committed by public officials. Cases in our records include jail breaking, abandonment of public office, refusal to accept posts in the *municipio,* embezzlement of public funds and abuse of authority by a public official, including unjust jailing, beating of prisoners and using a municipal post for personal, private gain against either the community or private persons.

A general comparison of Indian and Mestizo use of the district court will be presented after we discuss the ways in which Indians and Mestizos perceive and use their own local courts.

Mestizo Use of the Court: The Town of San Juan

The Mestizo residents of San Juan utilize the services of the court for multiple purposes. In fact, the town itself uses the court with a proportionally much higher frequency than any other community in the district (22% of all district cases).

San Juan is divided into three major classes which are locally recognized and named. The top is an elite (*la gente de categoría*) comprising 10% of the town's population. This elite is arranged in corporate kindred groups recognized by the *apellido* (surname) of the founding male. The town, and the elite, are also divided into two opposing political factions, and the elite derives its position from a traditional (pre-Revolution) political and economic control of the district. This is done through complex business enterprises involving cash-crop production, wholesale and retail import and export, monopoly of irrigation water, control of market stalls and the election of town-municipal officers from among the elite's clients, or through their own achievement of high posts in the state government (cf. Hunt 1965). Below the elite are two other classes: a small, transitional group of the middle class (10% of the population) and a majority of the lower class.

The middle and lower classes use the court constantly, for public as well as private business (see Figure II). The high degree of illegitimacy (60% of all births), and the prevalence of common-law marriages and concubinage-based households (*casas chicas*) create conflicts over inheritance of property, as well as unstable family relations. Outside the elite, the only effective family units are nuclear and these are highly unstable. Furthermore, there are no formal, effective mechanisms for handling interpersonal conflict at the familiar level. Thus, an extremely large number of cases of cases of conflict over family property, adultery, rape, wife beating, inheritance of illegitimate versus legitimate children, etc., are regularly brought to court. Moreover, most injury and homicide cases are the result of either inheritance disputes or family conflict. Because the political situation between the two town factions is also unstable, a considerable number of cases are brought to court by members of the opposing political faction against town officers who are claimed to have overstepped their authority for personal gain.

Figure II. Types of Cases presented in the District Court by the People of the Municipio of San Juan (Mestizo)

Types of Case	San Juan (Town)			Other Towns in the Municipio of San Juan		
	Total No. of Cases	No. of cases per 1000 inhabitants	Percent	Total No. of Cases	No. of cases per 1000 inhabitants	Percent
Homicide	12	6.04	11%	19	2.37	27%
Injuries	31	15.61	28.5%	28	3.49	40%
OAP	10	5.04	9%	1	.125	1%
Property	31	15.61	28.5%	13	1.62	19%
Const. Authority	11	5.54	10%	1	.125	1%
Family	14	7.05	13%	8	1.00	12%
TOTALS	109	55	100%	70	8.74	100%

Another significant use of the court is for property cases. The bulk of these are *juicios de desposeción,* evictions, surveys of boundaries and mensuration of lands. *Juicios de desposeción* are secondary appeals for inheritance cases in which a person has been excluded as a legitimate claimant for part or all of the inheritable property of a deceased person. In a context in which most persons die intestate, leaving more than one apparent common-law spouse, and/or several illegitimate children, the high frequency of these cases is to be expected. The other types of cases are evidence of constant conflict over landed property and irrigated orchards. Good land, which in San Juan means irrigated land, is very scarce. The town has multiple forms of land tenure: *Ejido,* private, public corporate, private corporate, and communal. Most individuals (except the elite) do not have titles to the land. Their claims are

usually based on retroactive tax payments over a period from 10
to 20 years. Few of these claims are registered with the appropriate
bureaucratic office (*Registro Público de la Propiedad*). But all land
(except, theoretically, *Ejido* land) can be sold, rented and manipulated as property in the market. Thus, landed property generates
constant conflict (between renter and leaser, old claimant and new
farmer, etc.). In the case of fruit orchards, conflict issues primarily
because trees can also be sold, rented, or leased for the harvest
independently of the land on which they stand. Since fruit trees
are a major source of income for most townsmen, the complications
of property claims and transactions are frequent causes of the
disputes taken to court.

The different classes of San Juan, however, use the court differently. In terms of the local scene, the use of the court by the elite is
characteristic of Mestizo power manipulation. Many elite activities
are, from the point of view of national law, illegal. First, they sell
water for irrigation which is in theory under Federal control
through a local committee. Second, the pattern of succession in the
family business is based on mono-inheritance, usually of the firstborn son. Third, monopolization of land is acquired through
giving high interest loans for future harvests.

The elite seldom use the court officially and then mostly for
cases of considerable theft. Petty theft is regarded as a privilege of
the poor and seldom leads to any kind of negative legal sanction.
Thus employees at an orchard ranch are virtually expected to sell
some of the fallen fruit, or pick one or two trees, and store clerks
are expected to help themselves to a few cartons of beer. Only
larger theft, such as stealing of the day's cash receipts, cattle, or
expensive farm equipment is reported in court. This device is
primarily used as a sanction in itself, since charges are usually
dropped after a scolding by the judge; the offenders may not even
be fired, or may regain employment soon after.

The elite also use the judge, as a legal specialist, outside of court
in activities which are actually not permissible by law. First, to
ensure against inheritance according to the national law—which
enforces parcelling of property among children, and the lengthy

testamentary procedures—the heads of the elite families of San Juan instead prepare bills of sale arranged so that the future heir is in control of the property. To make them "legal" these are signed by the judge, but are neither entered in the books nor dated. (These are not made effective in the lifetime of the person to a) avoid conflict between offspring and b) maintain control of the property until the end.) Finally, the elite use the judge to notarize mortgages for which the securities are far more valuable than the loan. When real estate is acquired on the basis of foreclosure of these loans for failure to repay, the judge enters it separately from the mortgage, as a bill of sale.

For cases of the lower classes versus the elite, the judge acts not as an agent but as a mediator. Lower-class individuals seldom bring a case to court in the hope of winning, unless their opponent is an even match in wealth and power. Against the elite, a few cases are brought as harrassment. Faced with a court case which involves time and money and which a member of the elite could easily win by utilizing his personal connections outside town (at higher decision-making levels) the elite prefers to use the local judge or court officers to discuss settlement with the plaintiff; usually the charges are officially dropped. These procedures occur outside the courtroom. One example will suffice here.

Doña María, a widow, contracted for five consecutive years to sell the harvest of fruit from a few trees constituting her deceased husband's property. She sold these rights to a man in town and deposited the cash with Mr. X., the head of one of the larger stores in town, to invest for her at normal rates of interest. The agreement was verbal. After a year, faced with complications of health and the approaching wedding of a son, Doña María decided to dip into her invested savings and ask for her money back. The store owner then claimed to have invested the money poorly and to have lost it. Doña María then took the case to court. She had two witnesses, quite reluctant to support her but who nevertheless came to court with her. The judge did not officially summon Mr. X. Instead, he had an informal chat with him at his house the next day. The store owner acknowledged that he had received the money (which he had denied previously) but that he was reluctant to return it because he was short of cash at the time. He insisted that the money was secure and that the judge should convince Doña María to leave it in his custody. In court, a few days later, Doña María was officially informed of the new situation. She then proceeded to declare that she would take the case outside the district unless her money was returned. She said she could not be threatened, since "she had nothing to lose by trying."

At this point, Doña María made sure that the case became public knowledge and that it soon became a hot piece of town gossip. The judge intervened again, outside the context of the court, with the store owner. His entreaties and that of other family members of Mr. X, convinced the store owner that it was preferable to come to a peaceful arrangement, primarily because several other small investors, afraid for their own capital, had decided to claim their money back. Doña María was summoned (outside court). She agreed to receive the invested money back, without claiming the due interest, within one month. In exchange, she dropped charges, and was asked to make clear to those within town, with whom she had communicated the troubles, that the store owner had neither stolen her money nor refused to return it. Official court records show only the entry of the plaintiff, and a later statement dropping charges because of a "misunderstanding" cleared up personally and informally outside court. A written *amonestación* (admonishment) "to those who bring cases without sufficient cause" was also entered, but was never delivered to the plaintiff.

In several other ways the judge adjusts his behavior to local Mestizo norms. Neither he nor the *Agente* of the *Ministerior Público* will pursue murder cases in which the defendant has voluntarily exiled himself from the district. San Juaneros believe that exile per se is more than sufficient punishment in most cases of homicide. This explains, to a large extent, while so few of the many homicide cases (2.6%) entered in the books even end in orders of jailing or in a definite sentence.

At this point one may wonder if the behavior of the judge is another typical case of personal corruption. In the cases of homicide and dropped charges, the judge and officers justify their semi-official behavior on the grounds that the Mexican court system is overcrowded with cases and understaffed with personnel, and that this is a drain on national and state income. (The state of Oaxaca has one of the lowest budgets of any state in the nation.) He may argue that he is performing a service to the nation by settling out of court or avoiding prosecution. He also obtains, in some of these cases, gratuities to supplement his meagre salary. These, however, are not necessarily bribes, but are often legal fees for notarizing, witnessing, acting as legal advisor etc. The *mordida* (bribe), however, is not absent. Stern (1966) has pointed out that *mordidas* in Mexico do not necessarily function as bribes, but can be regarded as tips, as an "inducement to an official to exert his power in the interest of a client". Local custom sanctions the right to give and receive the *mordida*. From the point of view of the national bureaucracy, however, this sort of personal remuneration is indeed illegal and a sign of corrupt legal practice.

In the cases of outright illegal performances, as can be expected, we did not obtain full information from the judge or court officers themselves. But the San Juan elite is neither secretive nor silent about its behavior. This elite is tied by kinship, political clientship and economics to the national elite of the state and the capital. If a judge makes himself disagreeable, he is likely to be transferred to a lesser post within a short period of time. Other officers of the state are in the same situation (for example, a tax inspector for the federal government was demoted while we were in the field because he attempted to justly tax one of the town's dominant families). Under these conditions, judges and other officers of the court find it difficult to adhere to the letter of the law if they are to protect their careers. Instead, soon after arriving in a town, they acquire a local assistant, who is not officially a part of the court personnel, but a *meritorio* (a clerk on merits). He is paid from the court officer's own pocket. This assistant becomes an interpreter of local custom, a living "Who's Who" in the community, and a source of information on incomes and expected gratuities. This provides the officer with solid ground upon which to make safe discriminations about cases passing through the court, standard accepted procedures outside the books, etc. It is important for the judge that bad reports on him do not go to higher-level officers (through private patron-client chains which are outside his control) and that cases should not be taken to other agencies (a strategy left more or less intact from the colonial regime), all of which cast doubt on his competence. To avoid this, he reinterprets cases so that they conform to the law, uses his lieutenants to obtain crucial information, and settles many cases out of court to protect important local people as well as his own career.

The national bureaucracy understands these difficulties and, according to provisions built into the law, officers of the court are often transferred from one town to another. If they are not, they soon become immersed in elite affairs. They may marry into the town's elite, or acquire a common-law wife of local origin, buy land, occupy posts in the local sodalities, etc. At the time of our fieldwork the judge of San Juan had acquired a mistress by whom he had two children (he also had a wife and children in the state capital), and was contemplating investing in some sugarcane land in the *municipio*. Thus, such activities transform what in Wolf's terms (1966) is legally seen as an impersonal, dyadic, vertical contract between the individual and the state, into a multistranded, polydyadic horizontal coalition between the officer and local interest groups. Hence, it is necessary to point out that the function of the local court for the San Juanero Mestizos is primarily adjusted to the local social structure and prevalent cultural norms, not to the aims of the national segment of Mexico which creates and attempts to enforce the law.

Mexican lawmakers have been exceptionally aware of the demands of the cultures in which they operate (witness the homicide laws, most of which refer to murder by firearm or machete, or the laws providing for the inheritance of concubines). However, it is nearly impossible to incorporate into a system not based on precedent the high degree of local variation of customary law, custom or norm. Consequently, deviations from the letter of the legal code are frequent. Furthermore, the court as presently constituted is not an effective agent of local change for the national system, functioning outside its own legitimate frame as it often does. Changes in the law itself, however, can be brought about by accumulative pressure, as when the local-level courts bring certain types of appeals to higher courts or outside (non-judiciary) agencies for *amparo* or revision. Since colonial times, there has been a tradition in Mexico of a) taking legal cases to several government agencies simultaneously and b) granting special protection to injured parties to safeguard the rights of private individuals vis-à-vis the state. The first practice tests the law in cases of conflicting decisions; the second has given rise to the writ of *amparo*, (a constitutional suit of a summary nature brought by individuals when their rights have been violated by the law or by acts of the authorities). (For a brief discussion of the *amparo* and other procedures of protection against the court in Mexico, see Lambert 1963. For more specific discussions see the Deschamps 1958; Echanove 1949:229-248; and Leon 1951.) When a particular law or official act at the local levels appears to produce an unusual number of revision appeals or *amparos,* these become danger signs as to the effectiveness of the law, and it then rests with higher law-making levels to adjust the letter of the law to the cultural facts.

INDIAN USE OF THE COURTS: THE MUNICIPIO OF SAN JUAN ANDRES

One of the functions of the municipal officers of San Andres is to deal with court cases. In the cases which pass through its doors, the San Andres court reflects practically every type of conflict present in the community. San Andreseños believe that the court is a community service to be used whenever a person or group of persons feels injured. There are, however, other formal and informal mechanisms to solve conflict outside the legal context: consultation with the family elders, curing ceremonies, etc. Only if these fail does conflict reach the court. In cases of stalemate at lower levels, even petty cases can be taken to court if an individual feels personally dissatisfied with more informal solutions. Even though damages may be small, or the conflict of slight consequence, taking a case to court, whatever the final solution, "clears the air." One of our informants stated the situation clearly:

"If the court decides, the gossip stops, and then everybody knows that whatever was decided was correct. Sometimes I have made a case worse than I felt was justified, so I could take it to the authorities. Then I knew nobody could say I was acting badly."

Not all types of cases are taken to court with equal frequency (see Figure III). Family difficulties are usually solved by the elders of the extended family, which in San Andres is a localized ambilateral descent group.

Two types of conflict appear regularly, however, in the court context. In cases of elopement, when the female's family has no direct appeal to the groom's kinsmen (i.e., when there has been no preliminary petition for the bride, or exchange of presents, or visits to arrange the marriage), the woman's family takes the case to court to promote reconciliation between the youngsters, and to insure that a) the girl will be supported, and b) a formal marriage will take place as soon as possible. Unless the woman is not a minor (or is a widow, or divorced), these cases are always decided in favor of the plaintiff's child.

The other common type of case is husband-wife conflict, when the intervention of the extended family has not been sufficient to restore marital harmony. These cases usually end in the granting of a traditional divorce (over 60% of cases), with the wife receiving property and alimony according to the length of the marriage and the number of children born. In the rest of these cases, a formal reconciliation (at least temporary) is achieved in public.

Family life in San Andres is far from harmonious. Of cases brought to the municipal court 24% deal with family conflict, including adultery, elopement, desertion, etc. Moreover, of property cases and petty fights, many are between defendants and plaintiffs who are kinsmen. Since traditional Indian law has subtle and efficient ways of handling such cases, these are seldom appealed

Figure III. Types of Cases presented in the Municipal (Indian) and District (Mestizo) Court by the Municipio of San Andres (Indian)

| | JUZGADO OF SAN ANDRES | | | JUZGADO OF DISTRICT | | | | | |
| | Whole Municipio of San Andres | | | | | | Town of San Andres | | |
Type of Case	Total No. of Cases	No. of cases per 1000 inhabitants	Percent	Total No. of Cases	No. of cases per 1000 inhabitants	Percent	Total No. of Cases	No. of cases per 1000 inhabitants	Percent
Homicide	3	1.32	4.5%	13	6.00	50%	5	5.12	36%
Injuries	3	1.32	4.5%	4	1.84	15.5%	3	3.07	21%
O.A. Persons	5	2.31	7%	–	0	–	–	0	–
Property	26	11.99	38%	8	3.69	31%	6	6.14	43%
Const. Authority	11	5.07	16%	–	0	–	–	0	–
Honor or Stability of the Family	16	7.37	24%	1	.46	3.5%	–	0	–
Witchcraft	3	1.32	4.5%	–	0	–	–	0	–
Endogamy rules	1	.46	1.5%	–	0	–	–	0	–
TOTALS	68	31.16	100%	26	11.99	100%	14	14.43	100%

Population Municipio 2175
Cabecera 978 = 45%

further. But even if a case is unsatisfactorily handled at the municipal level, from the point of view of one of the parties, family cases are seldom (if ever) taken to the district court. Indians indicate that they do not take these cases to the distrcit court because "officers do not understand how family cases should be handled," i.e., they do not understand customary law; they cannot grant divorces on Indian common-law marriages; they accord no importance to evidence legitimate in Indian customary procedure (e.g. was a bride-price paid?); they charge more in costs (between fines and small bribes) than the average Indian household can afford; and they usually overpunish the culprit. Elopement, for example, which the Indian sees as a good cause for thrashing the couple, or a corrective speech, or a public statement on morals, may in the district court get a male culprit from six months to six years in prison and from 50 to 500 pesos in fines (Código Penal, Libro Segundo, Chapter VIII, and XV.)

The San Andreseños also dislike taking any type of case except murder to the district court. Since cash cropping and land sale have been introduced in San Andres, however, and a number of Mestizo cattle ranches have been established in the area, property conflict has become endemic (38% of municipal court cases; 31% of cases taken to the district court). Plots which were once communal are now ambiguously treated as private property; e.g., coffee plants (the major cash crop) cannot be inherited in the same pattern as corn-planted land where the yearly harvest ends the life of the plant and closes the work cycle. The invasion of planted land by cattle owned by neighboring Mestizo ranchers is a constant source of disputes, and traditional Indian procedures (e.g. self help, rounding up of vagrant cattle, cutting animal ears) fail to provide solutions. Such cases (especially those involving Mestizos) are accordingly taken to the district court for appeal. Indians seldom, however, take cases involving municipal property or town jurisdictional conflicts because they believe that the Mestizos are either ignorant, are not interested in their vital land problems (and thus delay action) or are personally biased against the Indian community. These cases are not solved either at the municipal or district level, but are taken directly to higher courts, or to influential persons in the government, such as the governor of the state, the secretary of the President of Mexico, or the appropriate ministerial office.

During the time of our study, three cases were taken above the district level: one involving the property of the town school of one of San Andres' hamlets, one involving *Ejido* boundaries in the lowland section of the *municipio* bordering another town, and another involving political fission between two hamlets in the same municipal *Agencia,* followed by territorial conflict between them.

In all types of cases, the local authorities try to avoid over-punishment (one of the major threats to the Indian) by sending cases to district court with explicit instructions as to "how they should be treated." In one case of abandonment of office, for example, the municipal president sent a letter indicating that the *municipio* did not want the man jailed, but simply admonished and made to promise that he would not repeat the offense.

Two types of cases from San Andres are never taken to the district court: witchcraft cases, and those dealing with the transgression of endogamy rules. Indians know that endogamy regulations are outside Mexican law, and that "the judge does not treat witchcraft seriously, and Mestizos laugh about it" (sic). Indeed, witchcraft cases reaching the district court are not accepted for the records, or the charges are dropped or completely rephrased. Three cases taken to the district court from other towns exemplify the point. In one, a community brought complaint against a local witch who had failed to bring rain during a drought after the community householders paid him for his promise to do so. The district judge treated this as a case of fraud, and the fines were considered by many villagers to be far below the just cost of the loss of the corn crop. In two other cases individuals brought complaints: one desired protection as he had been unjustly accused of being a witch; the other desired protection against a man bewitching him. The first was treated as a case of libel, the second was dismissed, and the municipal officer accompanying the plaintiff and serving as witness was jailed for perjury and abuse of authority, although from the point of view of the Indian community he was simply performing his duty.

Other factors encourage the restriction of cases to the municipal level: In the village court, fines can be paid in kind or labor, an important consideration in an economy short of cash, while the officers of the district court are likely to laugh at, if not put in prison, a man attempting to pay a fine with a bag of corn. Indians tend to be unable to differentiate between taxation, fines, and tribute, primarily because other brokers who are government officials, especially travelling inspectors, will accept payments in goods which the Indian may believe are legal payments while in fact they are simply bribes to the official. Another factor is what Indians regard as arbitrary jailing. Occasionally, witnesses in a case may delay going to the district court when summoned, until some other important task (e.g. weeding a *milpa*) has been taken care of. In these cases, the district court officers may either fine the man or force his presence in court by sending an order of apprehension against him. Because of the frequent jeopardy to the witness himself, it is very hard for an individual to obtain witnesses for a district case. Since without witnesses a case may seldom be successfully resolved, there is little incentive to carry it to San Juan.

The types of cases which are automatically sent to the district court (unless the municipal officers dismiss them for lack of evidence) are murder or grave injuries involving attempted homicide. Homicide cases, in the Indian view, are sent to the outside because they rid the community of a vicious deviant. Even if a man is released from the district jail for lack of evidence, he has been publicly shamed and de facto exiled. Few of the culprits, Indians say, return to the village, primarily for fear of witchcraft or revenge murder. In fact, of several cases known to us, all the culprits withdrew to a local Mestizo-owned ranch notorious for welcoming such men, or moved to another state.

There are always at least two different views of the total picture in a bicultural situation. We have presented the Indian view in the previous pages. The Mestizo reaction, however, is equally important to complete the case. We have to understand that although the Indian and Mestizo segments of the society interact in many spheres of life, one of the characteristics of the system is that there is a great deal of structural ignorance about the workings of the "other" social segment. This is partially produced by the formal, impersonal contexts in which most interaction occurs; is partially the product of projection of bad traits into the "other" (i.e., ethnocentrism); and is partially caused by intrinsic contradictions in the morals, values, and view of man of Indians and Mestizos. Paradoxically, Mestizos regard Indians as both more evil and more virtuous than themselves (and vice versa). The participation of Indians in the district court system serves to reinforce Mestizo beliefs. The Indians of San Andres bring about the same proportion of homicide cases as Mestizos to the district court, and a negligible percentage of family cases, a pattern typical of case distribution in Indian communities. (The difference between Indian and Mestizo use of the court for family cases is significant at the .01 or better level.) From the point of view of the district court, therefore, Indians appear to bring a disproportionately large number of homicide cases. These ideas are widely found among Mestizos, and two popular conceptions about Indians find confirmation here: first, Indians are revengeful, violent and untrustworthy; second, they are loyal, loving and highly solidary in the midst of their families. Neither one of these beliefs is supported by actual patterns of behavior. First, family conflict is not rare in the Indian village; second, Indians do not have higher homicide rates than Mestizos.

The judge and the officers of the court, however, have a different interpretation: the Indians bring homicide cases because the law requires it; municipal authorities cannot keep long-term prisoners in the municipal jails; Indians do not know how to handle homicide cases, and fear revenge. On the other hand, Indians do not bring family cases because they are discouraged by the absolute refusal of the court to accept families rather than individuals as defendants.

The judge points out that, in any type of case, his primary difficulty is to make Indian witnesses understand that kinsmen are not equivalent or replaceable by each other in court. He has difficulty persuading them that wives cannot be brought to jail to bring back a runaway murderer, or a father cannot assign one of his sons to serve a jail sentence for him. The judge of San Juan also states that he dislikes the cases brought by Indians in which Indian common law and Mexican law are at odds. He finds them a wasteful expenditure of time and effort because he cannot avoid involvement in lengthy and heated discussions with Indians who constantly argue about points that, from their point of view, should be handled in different ways. His general attitude was that "Indian common law should be eradicated." Court officers apparently believe that by rejecting such cases they are promoting the death of the Indian legal system.

INTERFACE FUNCTIONS OF THE COURTS

We turn now to a consideration of the interface features of the courts in this region of rural Mexico. We have dichotomized the *municipios* of the district into Indian and Mestizo, and have claimed that they use the court system differentially. This proposition can be tested by a statistical handling of the cases recorded in the district court. In general, we suspected that 1) Indians would use the court less frequently than Mestizos, and 2) that whenever Indian customary law disagreed with or contradicted state and national Law, a smaller number of cases related to these laws would be brought to the district court by Indians than by Mestizos. More specifically, our hypotheses were:

1) Indians bring fewer total cases.
2) Indians bring the same proportion or more Homicide cases as Mestizos.
3) Indians bring fewer Injury cases.
4) Indians bring fewer Other Against Person cases.
5) Indians bring fewer Property cases.
6) Indians bring fewer Constituted Authority cases.
7) Indians bring fewer Family cases.

Before we proceded to test these hypotheses another factor had to be considered. We wanted to make sure that physical distance from the district capital did not account for differential use of that court. This could have been expected because of difficulties of communication in a region without mechanical means of transportation. We therefore ranked the *municipios* in terms of distance from San Juan by the number of hours of walking which were necessary to reach it, and correlated it with the rank order of cases per 1000 inhabitants (Kendall's Tau, −.17). The result was not statistically significant, and we consequently discarded distance as a significant factor.

The test of hypotheses 1-7 was conducted with the Kolmogorov-Smirnov one-sample test (Figure IV). It was found that Indians do use the district court proportionally less than Mestizos (68%, with 75% of the population, hypothesis 1 accepted at the .05 level of significance). The Indian towns, with 75% of the population,

Figure IV. Comparison of Proportion of Cases sent to District Court by Indian vs. Mestizo towns*

Type of Case	Total No. of Cases	Indian Towns No.	%	Mestizo Towns No.	%	No. of Expected Mestizo Cases	D	Sig level
Homicide	167	127	75%	40	25%	41.75	.0148	—
Injury	131	81	62%	51	38%	32.75	.139	.05
OAP	16	11	69%	5	31%	3.36	.103	—
CA	11	6	55%	4	45%	2.75	.114	—
Property	66	47	70%	19	30%	16.5	.378	.01
Family	28	12	43%	16	57%	7.0	.321	.01
TOTAL	420	284	68%	136	32%	105	.0738	.50

Indian = 75% of population, Mestizo = 25%
Mestizo frequencies include only San Juan's proportion of District cases (c.f. pp. 12-13).

* Kolmogorov-Smirnov one-sample test (Siegel 1956:47-52)

bring 75% of all homicide cases to the district court (hypothesis 2 was accepted). Injury, Property and Family cases are also proportionally small (Hypotheses 3, 5 and 7 accepted respectively at the .05., .01 and .01 level). Others Against Persons and Constituted Authority were in the predicted direction, but were not significant statistically.

We have, therefore, concluded that the numerical data strongly support our statements that the Indian and Mestizo segments of the population make differential use of the district court. Furthermore, differences fall according to predictions based on ethnographic analysis and preliminary inspection.

In terms of the Indian segment, the municipal court functions to maintain and foster cultural and social separation at the local level. Since important decisions involving the basic normative structure of the community do not go to the outside, the outcomes do not test or challenge customary law vis-à-vis national law, nor do they foster behavioral change or acculturation. The kinds of conflict which are not handled at the municipal level are sent to either the district court (which drains the local community of some conflict), or directly to a high national office or institution. The municipal court helps to maintain stability in the local social system partly because it can resolve many standard conflicts at the local level (without interference from the higher level courts, which operate with a different law) and partly because it has those higher courts to refer insoluable conflicts to, thus relieving the Indian corporate entity of responsibility for them.

The municipal court thus functions as an important interface link in the communication network between the local Indian and the national segments. On the one hand, it is an institution in which is stored a considerable amount of information about the legal structure of both the local and the national society. On the other, it is a filter for legal cases reaching the nationally oriented courts. Further, the local court is one of the two major junctures of national and Indian law because, while all judicial officials are supposed to apply only federal and state law, the municipal court often applies local customary law to the Indian cases.

But the national system in fact has sovereignty over the local communities. Because it has a monopoly on force, it can compel acceptance of decisions which are contrary to local law, when it seems important to do so. There are, therefore, national-system constraints which the local segment must adapt to, and the municipal court serves to ameliorate the impact. The contrast between the treatment of homicide and family cases shows how the courts serve to stabilize the Indian community as a separate sociocultural system.

From the Indian point of view the district court is an unsatisfactory place to seek a resolution of conflict. As we pointed out, it is expensive and humiliating to take a case to that court. This reinforces the Indian awareness of his own, special cultural status, and keeps him dependent upon traditional means for resolving conflict.

The district court also functions at the interface. Like the municipal court, it is also a juncture of national and local law. Its brokers (the court personnel) are often made uncomfortable by the disparity between the two cultures. The judge and the officers of the court see themselves as performing a thankless service. In fact, while we were in the field the secretary of the court resigned to move to another town in the hope that he would not have to deal with Indians and thus could make a better living.

Unlike the ordinary Mestizos, the court personnel are fairly knowledgeable concerning customary Indian law, but their inability to yield to it encourages the Indians to resolve traditional disputes within the confines of their own communities. The district court is thus a conservative interface institution, in that it functions to maintain cultural differences between the two social segments. We might just point out that the judge of the district court of San Juan applies national standards more rigorously to the Indians than he does to the Mestizos who use him for conflict resolution. Thus, the ability of Indians and Mestizos to manipulate the legal apparatus is unequal.

For the local Mestizo, vis-à-vis the Indian, the district court provides an indicator of his difference from and superiority to the Indian world, and for the national bureaucracy and its brokers the court functions as a reaffirmation of the marginality of the Indian culture in terms of the mainstream of national life.

The situation clearly fits Bohannan's (1965) definition of colonial law and its working misunderstandings. In terms of its official definition, the Mexican court system is what Bohannan calls a municipal system. From the top, at the national level, the legal codes are built on the assumption that the legal system deals with one culture (i.e. national, Mexican) within a single state (unicentric power). In fact, the court system is centralized, but with two or more cultures with "greater or lesser problems of conjoining . . . and more or less overt theories of accomplishing the conjunction." In Mexico, as distinguished from Kenya or other overt forms of colonial rule, courts are not officially separated into distinct hierarchies, but formally appear to be centralized. But law as handled at the level of the municipal courts, and law as handled at the level of the district, state and national courts, are greatly out of phase. Custom and law at the municipal level are less out of phase than customary Indian law and national law. Why this should be the case can be explained in Wolf's (1966) terms, by pointing out that the local municipal courts function in a context of multistranded polyadic horizontal networks, and checks against its being out of phase are multilateral. The district court, on the contrary, functions for the Indian in a single stranded, dyadic vertical mode and its links with the rest of the Indian social system are thus very tenuous.

The discovery that Indians are, in terms of the court systems, members of internal colonies is not surprising. Internal colonialism has been, in fact, pointed out for Mexico in other contexts (e.g., Gonzales Casanova 1965). In the national court system, as in other areas, the Indian represents a marginal population of internal colonies. For the rural Mestizos, who are provincial but nevertheless integrated into the national scene, the court, like other aspects of the social system, can be manipulated both from within and from without. Polyadic, many stranded horizontal modes of interaction can be complemented, changed or upset by either dyadic single stranded vertical relations and dyadic or polyadic, many stranded vertical coalitions, all of which can affect the functioning of the legal apparatus.

In the light of this complex picture of checks and balances, of avoidances and structural ignorance, one should not be surprised to find that the role of the court is most significant when it does not appear to be involved.*

* Fieldwork upon which this paper is based was conducted in Mexico for 15 months during 1963-1964, and was generously supported by NSF with their grant GS-87. The original idea for focussing fieldwork on the court system came from a remark by Julian Pitt-Rivers during the Chiapas Seminar of the University of Chicago in 1962. (See Julian Pitt-Rivers, "Wards and Deeds: The ladinos of Chiapas," *Man*, 2:71-86, 1967.) He suggested that the Court officers in the community of Ocosingo, Chiapas, reinterpret witchcraft murder cases to fit the frame of Mexican law (later published in Pitt-Rivers, 1967:83). We are grateful to Lilo Stern for carefully reading and extensively commenting upon an earlier version. The responsibility for this version is, of course, ours alone.

EDWARD P. DOZIER

Peasant Culture & Urbanization: Mexican Americans in the Southwest

The Spanish-speaking populations found today in the urban areas of the Southwestern United States have been drawn from various sources. It is customary, for example, to delineate three main groups of these people: the Mexican-Americans, who are United States citizens and longtime residents of Texas, Arizona and California; the descendants of the sixteenth- and seventeenth-century colonists in New Mexico, often called "Hispanos"; and the recent immigrants or "Newcomers" (Burma 1954:35 fn. 1, McWilliams 1945:117, Saunders 1954:44-63). Some differences may be noted among all those groups, yet it is also possible to focus on those traditional institutions, behavioral norms, key values and beliefs which are shared by them. There is agreement among scholars on these shared patterns. This paper will 1) present the generic characteristics of Mexican-American society and culture, 2) note some of the more striking changes which are taking place as these people move into new environments, and 3) provide explanations for these changes.

All Mexican-American groups in the Southwest have a fairly recent "peasant" background despite their present locations in predominantly urban areas. This does not mean that Mexican-Americans are urban peasants, but that historic roots in a peasant culture continue to have important influences on contemporary

Mexican-American society and culture. A succinct characterization of peasant cultures in Latin America is contained in a paper by Wagley and Harris (1955:431-433):

> Throughout Latin America, the people who inhabit rural farms and the numerous small and isolated agricultural villages have a way of life which is analogous in many respects to that of peasants in other parts of the world. . . . Peasant type subcultures [in Latin America] are characterized by a predominance of archaic European patterns, which survive alongside the American Indian or African patterns and which are slowly giving way to new national patterns and institutions. Although [peasants] tend to be regional in their loyalties and to have but a vague idea of what it means to be a member of a nation, national patterns and institutions play a larger role in Peasant than in Modern Indian subcultures. . . .

HISTORY

The Hispanos of New Mexico and southern Colorado have resided in the United States much longer than any other Spanish-speaking group. These people are the descendants of settlers who accompanied the original colonizer, Juan de Oñate, and other colonizing expeditions into New Spain in 1598. Although they had already become mixed with Indians in Mexico, they held themselves aloof from local Indian populations in New Mexico. The Hispanos lived close to Pueblo Indian communities and other settlements of Indians, called "Genizaros" who had been bought or ransomed from Comanche, Ute, Apache, and Navaho Indians, (Adams and Chavez 1956:42, fn.71). During the latter part of the nineteenth century the Genizaro populations were absorbed by the Hispanos, but intermarriage between Hispanos and Pueblo and other Indians has been minimal. Although a mixed group biologically, culturally the Hispanos contrast sharply with their Indian neighbors; theirs is an Hispanized culture in which medieval Spanish characteristics are strong.

Over a period of two or more centuries, as Spain's power declined and contact with the seat of government in Mexico all but disappeared, the Hispanos carried on an isolated cultural existence. The mountainous region of northern New Mexico, where most of the Hispanos live, has not been an area of industrial development or of large-scale farming operations. In recent years much of the population has been drained away to urban areas like Albuquerque or out of the state to Denver, Chicago, Los Angeles, and San Francisco. Traditional Hispano culture, however, survives in villages (averaging from 200 to 250 inhabitants) which dot the Rio Grande Valley and tributary valleys from El Paso to southern Colorado (see Leonard and Loomis 1941, Sanchez 1940, United States Department of Agriculture 1935, Vol. 2).

Other Spanish-speaking settlements within the confines of the present United States came into existence at least a hundred years later. Those in the San Antonio region date from the establishment of the presidio during the second decade of the eighteenth century, and ranches on the lower Rio Grande Valley were founded somewhat later (Madsen 1961:5). In southern Arizona the presidio of Tucson was founded in 1776. During the first half of the nineteenth century, Mexican soldiers secured land grants and established cattle ranches in southern Arizona. During the middle of the nineteenth century, Apache raids forced the abandonment of these lands and the Mexican families retreated to Sonora, although a few settled in the presidio area of Tucson to form the nucleus of Tucson's Spanish-speaking population (see Getty 1949 and Tucson Project Statement). California received its settlers from Mexico with the establishment of the Franciscan missions in the latter part of the eighteenth century.

None of the Spanish-speaking populations in California, Arizona or Texas established the social and cultural solidarity of the Hispanos of New Mexico. Tucson and other parts of Arizona received a fairly large Mexican population after the Civil War and again in the period from 1910 to 1920. Arizona's present Mexican population is small compared to that of Texas and California; it is also overwhelmingly from Sonora (Tucson Project Statement). The large influx of Mexicans into Texas and California began during the second decade of this century, following the Mexican

Revolution in 1910, and coincided with the development of large-scale farming and the demand for cheap labor. These immigrants were chiefly from the central and northern plateaus in the states of Michoacan, Jalisco, Guanajuato, and Aguascalientes (Gamio 1930: 13; Tuck 1946:67). The majority of the present Mexican-American population descended from these immigrants is now native-born, U.S. citizens.

The 1960, Mexican-American population in the Southwest, calculated on the basis of Spanish surnames, was reported as follows: Arizona 194,356; California 1,426,538; Colorado 157,173; New Mexico 269,122; Texas 1,417,810 (U.S. Bureau of the Census, 1963). Except for the Hispanos of New Mexico, most of the Mexican-American population is concentrated in urban areas.

SOCIAL AND CULTURAL CHARACTERISTICS

It is obvious that Mexican-Americans in the Southwest have come from different areas and thus exhibit social and cultural diversity. It is possible, however, to isolate certain general patterns which tend to persist or change in characteristic fashion in new environments. These patterns are generic in the sense that they existed primarily in the past. Some may be "ideal" rather than "real," but in any case these patterns serve as important guidelines for behavior today and are thus crucial to understanding contemporary Mexican-American life.

THE VILLAGE

The most characteristic feature of traditional Mexican and Hispano life was (or is) the village. As Foster (1961:1177) puts it: "The basic, visible, identifiable segment is the village. It is there, a physical reality; it can be mapped; its inhabitants can be counted; one can walk around its limits." While Mexican-Americans in the United States may now live in urban environments, former village life is still alive in the memory of many.

The village plan could not be physically transported to the city, although in cities which have developed from former Hispano or Mexican towns, vestiges of the early settlement pattern often remain: the central plaza, the church, nearby public buildings and houses of prominent families, while grouped around the outskirts of the plaza are the homes of the villagers (see Foster 1960:34-49; Stanislawski 1947:95-105). In modified form the old town pattern remains as a central feature in Santa Fe, Taos, and Socorro, New Mexico, and El Paso, Texas. In Albuquerque, Los Angeles and San Antonio, where the city has grown in another part of town, the pattern of Mexican town has been retained only for historic and tourist interests.

The significance of the Mexican village- and town-settlement patterns is that social and religious institutions were an integral part of the compact village. In comparing the Hispanic American plaza to its Spanish counterpart, Foster (1960:48) remarks:

> Sociologically, the Hispanic American plaza is far more important than the Spanish plaza. The former is the geographical as well as the cultural center of a community, where the evening promenades take place, where the major stores front, adjacent to which, or even in which, will be found the open market. Life seems to swing about these central focal points. In Spain, with rare exceptions, plazas almost seem to be avoided. Fashionable promenades follow strees in the cities, and the hub of the community lies away from the plaza.

Villages in Mexico—and those which are historically deeply rooted in the Southwest—are (or were) corporate entities. A few Mexican villages were given charters by King Charles V of Spain early in the sixteenth century, but even towns without formal charters developed and operated as independent units. An individual had legal membership by virtue of being born in the village. A person who has lived a long time in a village in which he was not born may claim it as his own, but he is always aware that he is not a native and the fact is constantly made clear to him by the behavior of his fellow villagers. Village membership, not kinship affiliation or extraterritorial membership, is the basis of identification. Further, except for the *patrón* and his family, differences in socioeconomic or prestige statuses are of minor importance.

Besides the village, the following institutions and relationships are the fundamental structural features of Mexican society: the *patrón* system, the church, the nuclear family, the *compadrazgo* system, and neighbors. The church and the *patrón* system are institutions through which the village is related to the outside, but other relationships operate almost completely within the village and among those individuals who share socioeconomic equality. These institutions and relationships provide the village with integration and give it an independent, autonomous orientation. Traditional Mexican villages, whether in Mexico or the Southwestern United States are, of course, part of a higher political system at both the state and national levels. In the past, state and federal officials in the United States and Mexico seldom interfered with village affairs, either through respect for the autonomous character of these villages or perhaps simply from a lack of interest. Routine civil matters and incidental secular affairs involving the outside were usually satisfactorily handled through the *patrón,* while the local priest functioned analogously in matters concerning church affairs. The villagers, for their part, were content to be left alone and to let the *patrón* and priest take care of the complicated and often disturbing matters that came in from outside the village.

THE PATRÓN SYSTEM

Mexican dependency relationships are crucial to an understanding of the problems of adjustment which Mexicans face as they move into urban life and as modern changes penetrate into rural areas. The *patrón* relationship consisted of a system of reciprocal obligations between one man and village members. Members of the *patrón's* family were treated with respect and deference. A *patrón's* position was inherited by his firstborn son, and the position was thus passed along the male line. The *patrón* was usually a large landowner, often the descendant of the prominent Mexican who had originally acquired the grant of land on which the village stood. Where villages developed without any land grants, the *patrón* might be anyone of wealth or prestige. In return for services supplied, villagers worked on the *patrón's* lands and assisted him in many other endeavors with little or no compensation.

In New Mexico a *patrón's* clients were expected to support his political party and, if the *patrón* himself ran for an office, to vote for him. Florence R. Kluckhohn (1961:177) has described the New Mexico *patrón* system admirably in her study, "Spanish-Americans of Atrisco":

> The average man and woman in the villages voted, but whom he or she voted for was not a matter of individual choice unless the voter wished to suffer the dire consequences of a *patrón's* disfavor. The average villager had no basis upon which to make a choice even had he wanted to assert his rights. Anglo-American politicians, even when they had wider interests than making mutually advantageous deals with the Spanish-American leaders, seemed simply to assume that it was either the business of the *patrón* to educate the people of a village in the ways of democratic government or the business of the people somehow to educate themselves. It was not much to their own interests to labor with the problem. And it certainly was not to the interest of the *patróns* who could see only a threat to their own power in a voting public which was well enough educated in democratic procedures to make independent choices. The result of this situation was the development in New Mexico of a type of machine politics which has often been vicious and sometimes ludicrous. [Cf. Edmonson 1957:45]

The *patrón* system as described above was most commonly associated with small village populations, small scale farming, and operating cattle and sheep ranches. Large land holdings were common in Mexico before the turn of the century; but the *hacendado*, or landlord, was no counterpart of the *patrón*, although he was addressed as such by the peons during his rare appearances at the hacienda. The *hacendado* was usually an absentee landlord who lived on his hacienda for only short periods of time and left the management of his estate to a foreman or *mayordomo*. The peons who worked on the hacienda were virtually slaves and never developed the kind of relationships of mutual obligation, help and service described above. The dependency factor was there, however, especially in indebtedness to the *mayordomo* for the simple necessities of life. The land reforms which swept Mexico during the Revolution of 1910 virtually destroyed the hacienda type of landholdings, and a whole way of life completely disappeared (Whetten 1948:90-107).

Another type of *patrón* relationship has been established in the Southwest with Anglos who either marry Mexican-Americans or who become familiar with the operation and benefits of the *patrón* system and engage in it. Not all Anglos who come into a relationship with the system understand it or can exploit it advantageously, but those who can operate successfully in the system assume the same kind of obligations and receive like rewards from their Mexican-American clients as have been traditionally accorded to prominent Mexican individuals. (See Kluckhohn and Strodtbeck 1961:249-251; Romano 1960:968-969).

THE CHURCH AND THE CATHOLIC PRIEST

The most prominent building in a Mexican village is the Catholic church. The larger villages (or the more centrally located village in a group of villages) have a resident priest, and at least one mass is offered in the church every day. Other villages may be visited only on Sundays or holy days, while more distant villages may not get a visit except monthly and on the patron saint's feast day. Marriages, baptisms and confessionals are timed to the priest's visits. For funerals it is necessary to send for the priest, though simple burial services for young children are often conducted by a layman.

The Catholic priest occupies an important position in the social status system of Mexican villages. He is most often consulted on religious matters, but his influence in the secular domain is often intense and broad. Depending on his personality and ambitions, a priest's leadership in those villages under his jurisdiction may be profound (see Beals 1946:119; Lewis 1951:260-263). His influence may overshadow that of the *patrón* and villagers may thus come to him to discuss both religious and secular affairs. But the *patrón* and the priest usually complement one another. In cases where a priest visits a village infrequently, the *patrón* assumes some of the religious roles. If there is no church, the *patrón* may offer his home for religious services, or may even use his own funds to build a church. Prayers and other services which do not require a priest might also be conducted by the *patrón* or his wife.

Anti-clerical attitudes are common in Mexico. They are often produced by interference in the local customs of a village. It is not uncommon for particular priests to be severely criticised and demands are frequently made to higher authority for their removal. Nevertheless, in many villages the priests have acted as buffers against the intrusion of the outside world and worked as liaisons between villagers and the outside (cf. Beals 1946:119; Francis 1956; Lewis 1951:260-263).

The village church, both as a structure and a symbol, is the pivotal point for another sphere of village activity and for the integration of its members. The church houses the images of saints, or *santos,* in particular the Virgin Mary and the patron saint. Annually, a religious festival—the *fiesta*—is held in honor of the patron saint (Compa 1932; Kurath 1949). In addition, there may also be another saint who is similarly honored at another time of the year with a less elaborate but nevertheless important fiesta. Other religious festivals are associated with Holy Week, All Saints Day and All Souls Day, and Christmas. On all of these occasions the church is the starting point of activities. These events are as much social as religious affairs, and they provide a release of tension from the rather humdrum routine of day-to-day existence (cf. Redfield 1930:91-92, comment on festivals in Tepotzlan, Morelos, Mexico).

Other occasions of social and religious significance marked by a feast are the life-cycle events recognized by the Church. These are associated with the coparent or *copadrazgo* system, described below. Such occasions as baptism, first communion, confirmation, marriage and death entail either a selection of ceremonial sponsors or the participation of these sponsors in prescribed duties and rites. All such occasions have social and recreational functions as well as religious ones. Weddings are always followed by a feast and a dance in the evening. Other life-cycle events may not have a dance, but an elaborate meal for family members, godparents, neighbors and friends is usually an important feature of all such occasions. Even the wake at a funeral has its pleasurable side. Men congregate around a fire outside the home where the death watch is being held. Here, while a bottle of whiskey is passed around, stories and jokes are told. Early in the morning, before daylight, a meal is set out for all those who have remained the night through.

In the United States these sociocultural characteristics of the Mexican-American people have been modified. No longer are Mexican villages—either in Mexico or the Southwest—as isolated as they were two and three decades ago. Improved economic conditions, the automobile, the construction and improvement of roads, the spread of modern communications systems—all have had their influence. Because of the villagers' greater awareness of the outside world, the power of the *patrónes* has been weakened or destroyed completely. Catholicism is not as strong as it formerly was; Protestant missionaries have converted a few individuals or families in virtually all villages; and disbelievers and nonconformists have also risen. In addition, in the Southwestern United States the control and organization of the Catholic church is now in the hands of Anglos, few of whom speak Spanish. While the church authorities attempt to assign Spanish-speaking priests to Mexican villages, it has not always been possible to do so. Often, then, a village or group of villages is served by priest of a different ethnic background, who speaks little or no Spanish, and has little understanding of Mexican-American society and culture. The traditional dependency relationship upon the priest has thus either disappeared or become substantially weakened. Mexican-Americans also hesitate to use the services of counselors and social workers who would appear to have superceded, in large part at least, the functions originally performed by the church and the village priest. Undoubtedly the reason for failing to achieve a satisfactory transference is that counselors and social workers are invariably Anglos. Until Mexican-Americans themselves fill these positions in their neighborhoods, language and cultural barriers will prevent the full use of the services provided by these agencies.

FAMILY

So far we have described relationships which bound (or bind) villagers with the outside. Those to be discussed now are internal to the community or neighborhood The most important institution is that of the family. While the kind of family from which Mexican-American residents of the Southwest originally came (whether from Mexico or New Mexico) is similar, there are some differences which need to be noted in order to understand the nature of this unit in the urban environment.

Accounts of the family in central Mexico describe it as a nuclear unit with little or no extension. The household typically contains one or two other close relatives besides the nuclear family, but it is not as large as its Hispano counterpart. Postmarital residence is customarily patrilocal, i.e., a bride usually, but not always, joins the groom in his home. Commonly, a separate residence is constructed when the first child is born, and thus a new nuclear-family household is formed. There is some tendency for sons to build homes near that of their parents, but this is not a rule. Male dominance in the family is strong, but women have a lot to say in the household, and are by no means intimidated by males. While all land belongs in theory to the village, it is actually individually owned; men and women generally have equal rights of inheritance. Husband and wife pool their land resources to support themselves and their children, but individual rights to land are not surrendered to either spouse and are independently passed on to the children.

Descriptions of the New Mexican Hispano family in the village setting generally agree with the above description. But the Hispano family unit appears to be larger and somewhat more male dominated than those reported for central Mexico.

Family roles among Hispanos also emphasize male authority and respect for older kin. The husband is the head of the household and his wife and children owe him obedience and respect. Even after the children have grown and have established separate residences, interaction with a parent demands obedience and respect. A woman's place is in the home, and the wife must be faithful and submissive to her husband. Brothers and sisters are expected to help one another and provide moral support. In all kin relationships deference is shown to age and male sex. The oldest brother, or *hermano mayor,* is accorded special attention for he is the heir to his father's authority and position as head of the family (cf. Edmonson 1957:27-33; Foster 1961:1181; Kluckhohn and Strodtbeck 1961:192-204; Lewis 1951:319-346; Saunders 1954:48; Burma 1954:8-9).

The above descriptions are ideal or expected forms of behavior; actual practices may deviate widely from these patterns. Perhaps conformity to the ideal pattern was closer in the traditional Hispano family where face-to-face relations in small village populations were almost daily occurrences. Elsewhere in Hispanic America, although there may be outward compliance, there are numerous deviations from the expected roles of family members (see Foster 1961:1181; Lewis 1949:602-610; 1951:319-346).

THE COMPADRAZGO SYSTEM

Cooperation in a wider social, economic and ritual context on the village level is accomplished largely through the *compadrazgo* system (cf. Beals 1946:89-90 and 100; Foster 1961:1179; Lewis 1951: 58-79; Parsons 1936:66-70 and 545-551). This institution appears to be more complexly developed in central Mexico than among Hispanos or other Mexican groups in the Southwest. *Compadrazgo* is a fictional kinship system established by the selection of a sponsor or a pair of sponsors on certain occasions in an individual's life. The system is ordinarily fitted to the life-cycle rites of the Catholic church, but in many groups the system prescribes more sponsors and recognizes additional occasions not specified by the church. Three classes of individuals are involved in the system: 1) the initiate; 2) the parents of the initiate; and 3) the ceremonial sponsor or sponsors. Terms used between and among these sets of relatives are much the same everywhere since they stem from Spanish usage; the expected behavior of the individuals so bound is also remarkably alike everywhere in Hispanic America. The initiate, called *ahijado* (male), *ahijada* (female), refers to his sponsors as *padrino* (male) and *madrina* (female), or collectively as *padrinos*. The initiate's parents and sponsors are referred to collectively as *compadres*, but call each other *compadre* (male), *comadre* (female).

In its simplest form, the *compadrazgo* provides for the selection of sponsors on the following occasions: two sponsors, one of each sex for the rite of baptism; one of the same sex as the initiate for confirmation; and two, one of each sex, for marriage. In Hispanic America the *compadrazgo* has been elaborated from this simple base by two procedures: 1) selecting an additional sponsor or pair of sponsors for each event, or 2) increasing the number of occasions on which sponsors are selected. Catholic priests serving Spanish-speaking groups are either ignorant of the church ruling on the *compadrazgo* which restricts the number of sponsors or else they have permitted villagers to abuse the system. At any rate, the number of sponsors and occasions on which sponsors are chosen have been expanded among virtually all Spanish-speaking groups in the New World (cf. Gillin 1947:105; Parsons 1936:68-69 and 228; Spicer 1940:91-116, 1954:58-62). It occurs in elaborated form in central Mexico (see Beals 1946:12; Gamio 1930:13; Tuck 1946:67). The Hispanos of New Mexico, however, follow the simple form specified by the Church. The system among these people emphasizes the relationship between godparents and godchildren (see Kluckhohn and Strodtbeck 1961:182; Hawley and Senter 1946:138), whereas in Mexico the relationship between godparents and the godchild's parents is stressed (cf. Foster 1953b:7).

The extended family and the *patrón* system in New Mexico

appear to serve the functions provided by the *compadrazgo* in central Mexico. The latter is present in the Hispano villages, but in weaker form. The reason that the *compadrazgo* remained unimportant may be simply that in the isolated small villages of New Mexico is was far easier in crises situations to appeal to one's extended family (sometimes the whole of a village) and to the powerful, benevolent, *patrón* and his family than to classificatory or ritual kin. Both the *compadrazgo* and the *patrón* systems are institutions which provide solace to villagers in time of economic need or when troubled by social, psychological or religious problems. Pioneer conditions among the Hispanos, where populations were small, have apparently made the *patrón* system a more appropriate institution for providing many of the same functions served by the *compadrazgo* in the far more densely populated and ecologically varied environment of central Mexico. Both institutions were present in the two areas but the importance and elaborateness of each system differed. Indeed, all the differences between the social relationships and institutions in central Mexico and the frontier areas of the North are essentially matters of degree and emphasis— all Mexican groups had or have the same basic institutions.

NONKINSHIP UNITS

All of the village institutions discussed thus far are based on kinship, either biological or, as in the case of the *compadrazgo,* ritual or fictitious. One of the significant things about Mexican village life is the virtual absence of nonkinship associations. In Spain, Foster (1953b:2-3) has noted that while the *compadrazgo* was important up to the medieval period, in later times it was the nonkinship units of the *cofradia* (brotherhoods) and the *gremio* (guilds)—or more properly, a combination of these organizations— which became the primary basis for relationships outside the family. The *cofradia* and *gremios* were also introduced into Hispanic America, and we have some vestigial units which apparently represent the partial incorporation of these organizations into some communities, but generally such organizations have not become major features in the Mexican rural villages. The *Penitente* cult of the Hispano village resembles Spanish-type *cofradias,* as do the *Mayordomias* of Central Mexico.

The *penitente* cult is a religious brotherhood organization among the Hispanos. It was formerly of great importance, with members in virtually all the villages. During Holy Week its members reenacted the passion of Christ and flagellated themselves. At other times the cult was a mutual help organization. Its members helped in burial rites and provided solace and comfort to the bereaved family of the deceased. Although the penitente cult undoubtedly developed from a *cofradia,* it is not at present an approved organization of the Catholic Church. (For information about the cult, see Chavez 1954; Edmonson 1957:33-35.)

It is significant that as kinship ties, either actual or ritual, break down in the Southwestern United States, Mexican-Americans form nonkinship organizations such as social and business clubs. These are obviously attempts, largely unconscious, to find substitutes for traditional institutions which cannot function properly in the urban environment.

VALUES

Emphasis on family and family background is closely associated with identity or self image among Mexicans. To be of *un buen familia* (a good family) is an important mark of status and self-esteem. A major aspect of the stress on proper family affiliation and background is to deny or to look down on any American Indian admixture (that is, obvious or recent admixture). This is a curious anomaly for, of course, Mexicans come from a Mestizo background, where Indian physical traits are often dominant. This denial of a mixed ancestry, coupled with the inability to recognize and lay claim to a cultural heritage of their own, has produced in the Mexican (according to some Mexican writers on Mexican character) what has been described as a sense of "inferiority" or "insufficiency," as well as a self-destructive temperament (see Paz 1947; Pineda 1959, 1961; Ramirez 1959; Ramos 1962:4-14; Sandoval

1951:112-126; Uranga 1949:135-148). Although Mexican writers disagree about the origin of this feeling, one line of development, which Hewes (1954:217) traces from a review of the literature on the subject, seems plausible:

The Conquest was a kind of psychic trauma, in which almost no native values were preserved; the arrogant [Aztec] ruling class and its priesthood were humiliated and forced into common subjection along with their former subjects. A national inferiority complex was thus born, to be nurtured for three centuries of Colonial domination. The new overlords and their clergy were perhaps actually less demanding than the ancient ones, but history provides abundant evidence that native tyrannies are far more tolerable than foreign oppressors. The growing Mestizo element in the population suffered even more than the legally protected Indian communities, and was further stigmatized with being the product of casual liaisons of Spanish men and Indian women.

Hewes further notes that some Mexican writers associate a stress upon male virility with the need to support a shattered ego. Ramos (1962) and Iturriago (1951) depict the Mexican male as a downtrodden *pelado* (literally "plucked," but the term has come to mean "a nobody"). The *pelado* is full of resentment and hostility and suffers from a feeling of inferiority, deriving satisfaction only in the belief that he is *muy macho*, very virile. He reacts constantly with verbal and physical violence, venting his resentment on others. While male dominance is undoubtedly a traditional aspect of Mexican folk culture, extreme forms of *machismo* appear in urban environments and reflect, perhaps, conditions of poverty, psychological deprivation, and social demoralization. Since the Mexican Revolution, despite some government attempts to glorify the Indian past (the policy known as *Indigenismo*), most Mexicans still look down on the Indian.

The dominant attitude of Mexicans toward girls and women is that they are weak, prone to evil, and hence must be watched and protected. Unmarried girls are escorted by older women or relatives when they go outside the house, and a boy may visit a girl or his fiancée only in her home where she is properly chaperoned. The wife is cloistered, while the husband may have mistresses or a series of extra-marital affairs. Fallen or evil women are those who have not followed the strict old mores; they can never hope to find a husband from a "buena familia" and may become outcasts with only the life of a mistress or a prostitute open to them. The sense of honor is associated on the one hand with the theme of *buena familia* and on the other hand with the Mexican concept of individualism (cf. Beals and Humphrey 1957:23). A Mexican must be ready to defend the good name of his family and must be ready to assist his relatives in time of need.

CHANGES AND INTERPRETATION

We have discussed the social and cultural characteristics which are deeply imbedded in and common to all Mexican groups. Now we may examine the changes these patterns undergo in new environments. The order of the preceding discusion will again be followed.

The former peasant base of Mexican culture has been disrupted in the Southwest urban environment. We can no longer describe Mexican populations in terms of face-to-face relationships nor characterize their lives as exhibiting a slow tempo of change. They are now very much a part of urban existence, even though conflict in institutions, values and beliefs are everywhere evident and adjustments to the new conditions are not always apparent.

Dependency relationships, which once cushioned contacts outside the village, have not been successfully developed in new environments. Yet Mexican-American communities in urban areas tend to seek out prominent individuals, either Mexican or Anglo, in times of financial or personal distress (Tuck 1946:137; Tucson Project Statement). At times a *patrón* relationship of the type which existed among rural Hispanos is established. The relationship described by Romano (1960:968-969) between the owner of the brick factory in the Texas town of "Frontera" and the Mexican community is similar to patron-client relationships elsewhere in

Mexico. Leadership unfortunately is not always available in the urban areas, since the population is mobile and the benefits which might accure to the leaders are not well defined, yet the dependency characteristics of the Mexican population remain to hamper adjustments to new conditions.

The influence of the Church has also weakened in the cities. Priests serving Mexicans are frequently Anglos unfamiliar with the nature of Mexican culture. The church is no longer a center for the saints' day activities and festivals so important in Mexican village life. Thus a powerful integrating force has been removed in the new environment. Satisfactory substitute or compensatory institutions and relationships appear not to have been developed, although there are attempts to find adjustments through new organizations. Increasing numbers of Mexican-American families are joining Protestant religious sects, and Tucson in particular is rife with Mexican-American social and business clubs. The impermanent nature of these organizations indicates, however, that none of these experiments has satisfactorily fulfilled the economic, social and psychological functions performed by the traditional Mexican organizations and relationships.

In south Texas (Madsen 1964:44-47) the extended family seems to be strong, but in other urban environments it has been reduced to the nuclear type. There are tendencies everywhere for a wider interaction and cooperation with aunts, uncles, and grandparents, but these relatives ordinarily live in separate households and are most often on the maternal rather than the paternal side. The Tucson Project Study and other studies have also revealed a large number of matrifocal-type households where the father is temporarily or permanently absent from the family. Such households frequently develop in areas where men are unable to find employment. If the wife must work to supplement the family income, conflict soon develops. As the husband's feelings of unimportance, displacement, inferiority, and doubted manhood increase, he may turn to "macho" activities as a defense against the feelings of inadequacy. The wife, on the other hand, assumes more and more responsibility and becomes the primary source of financial and emotional support for her family (see Landman 1953:141-144). Eventually the husband abandons the family.

All the traditional institutions and relationships of Mexican society have thus undergone major changes. The *patrón* system has virtually disappeared, the church and the fiesta system have weakened, and the family has shrunk into the nuclear form (or, in many instances, has become further fragmented into a matrifocal type). The *compadrazgo* system, too, has largely lost its importance and effectiveness in the urban environment. The Anglo clergy and church organization have reduced the rites to those recognized by the Church, and the godparent-godchild relationship rather than the compadre-comadre relationship has come to be emphasized. In the process, the psychological, social, and economic securities have been lost.

The study of the changes, shifts and reformations of social institutions and relationships, as well as of the concomitant adjustments in values, attitudes and beliefs, is of primary concern to sociologists and anthropologists. Of interest to all citizens are proper solutions to the problems of a population moving into a new situation. For all these interests, an understanding of the traditional social and cultural characteristics of the people under study and the more obvious changes which are taking place is imperative. We have attempted to present in this paper such a background for the Mexican-American population in the Southwest.*

* This paper is the result of a background study of Mexican and Mexican-American society and culture made as a part of the Southern Arizona Mental Health Project of the Department of Psychology, The University of Arizona. The project is being supported by a grant (No. 2RC-580(240)) from the U.S. Department of Health, Education, and Welfare, to which grateful acknowledgment is made. A preliminary version of this paper was read by the following: John H. Chilcott, Hans Leder, Malcolm and June McFee, Arnold Meadow, Octavio Ignacio Romano, Edward H. Spicer, and Roland Tharp. This paper has profited from their comments, but none of these individuals is, of course, responsible for its shortcomings.

Bibliographies

PHILIP K. BOCK: INTRODUCTION

Erasmus, Charles J.
    1961   *Man Takes Control.* Indianapolis, Bobbs-Merrill.

Foster, George M.
    1962   *Traditional Cultures and the Impact of Technological Change.*
           New York, Harper and Row.

Halpern, Joel M. and John Brode
    1967   "Peasant Society: Economic Changes and Revolutionary Trans-
           formation," *in* B. J. Siegal and A. R. Beals, eds., *Biennial Review*
           of Anthropology, 1967. Stanford, Stanford University Press.

Leach, E. R.
    1954   *Political Systems of Highland Burma.* Cambridge, Harvard Uni-
           versity Press.

Moore, Barrington, Jr.
    1966   *Social Origins of Dictatorship and Democracy.* Boston, Beacon
           Press.

Nash, June
    1967   "Death as a Way of Life: The Increasing Resort to Homicide in a
           Maya Indian Community," *American Anthropologist*, Vol. 69, No.
           5 (October, 1967), pp. 455-470.

Potter, Jack M., May N. Diaz and George M. Foster (eds.)
    1967   *Peasant Society: A Reader.* Boston, Little, Brown and Company.

Redfield, Robert
    1941   *The Folk Culture of Yucatan.* Chicago, University of Chicago
           Press.
    1953   *The Primitive World and Its Transformations.* Ithaca, Cornell
           University Press.
    1956   *Peasant Society and Culture.* Chicago, University of Chicago Press.

Steward, Julian (ed.)
    1967   *Contemporary Change in Traditional Societies.* Volumes I-III.
           Urbana, University of Illinois Press.

ROBERT BIRRELL

Bailey, F. G.
 1957 *Caste and the Economic Frontier.* Manchester, Manchester University Press.

Beardsley, R. K., Hall, J. W. and Ward, R. E.
 1959 *Village Japan.* Chicago, University of Chicago Press.

Bose, P.
 1962 Peasant Values and Innovation in India. *American Journal of Sociology,* March.

Boserup, E.
 1965 *The Conditions of Agricultural Growth.* Chicago, Aldine Publishing Company.

Chambers, J. D. and Mingay, G. E.
 1960 *The Agricultural Revolution 1750-1880.* London, B. T. Batxford.

Deane, P.
 1965 *The First Industrial Revolution.* Cambridge, Cambridge University Press.

Deane, P. and Cole, W. A.
 1962 *British Economic Growth 1688-1959.* Cambridge, Cambridge Unisity Press.

Dore, R. P.
 1959 *Land Reform in Japan.* London, Oxford University Press, p. 47.
 1965 Land Reform and Japan's Economic Development. *The Developing Economies,* vol. 3, no. 4.

Etienne, G.
 1968 *Studies in Indian Agriculture.* Berkeley, University of California Press.

Food and Agricultural Organization of the United Nations
 1967 "The Role of Agricultural Land Taxes in Japanese Development," in: *Readings on Taxation in Developing Countries.* R. M. Bird and O. Oldman, eds. Baltimore, The John Hopkins Press.

Fukutake, T.
 1964 Change and Stagnation in Indian Village Society. *The Developing Economics,* vol. 1, no. 2.
 1967 *Asian Rural Society: China-India-Japan.* Seattle, University of Washington Press.

Geertz, C.
 1963 *Agricultural Involution.* Berkeley, University of California Press.

Grigg, D.
 1966 *The Agricultural Revolution in South Lincolnshire.* Cambridge, Cambridge University Press.

Hammond, J. L. and Hammond, B.
   1927   *The Village Laborer*, London, Longmans, Green.

Hart, H. C.
   1967   *The Village and Developmental Administration*. Indiana, Comparative Administration Group, Occasional Papers.

Havinden, M. A.
   1967   "Agricultural Progress in Open-field Oxfordshire," in *Agriculture and Economic Growth in England 1650-1815*, ed. E. L. Jones. London, Methuen.

Heston, A.
   1968   Variations in Agricultural Growth and Output Between and Within Regions of India. *Asian Survey*, Vol. VIII, No. 3.

Hoskins, W. G.
   1957   *The Midland Peasant*. London, MacMillan.

Kawano, S.
   1965   Economic Significance of the Land Reform in Japan. *The Developing Economies*, vol. 3 no. 2.

Landes, D.
   1962   "Japan and Europe: Contrasts in Industrialization," in *The State and Economic Enterprise in Japan*, ed. William Lockwood. Cambridge, Princeton University Press.

Lewis, J. P.
   1964   *Quiet Crisis in India*. New York, Doubleday.

Lewis, O.
   1958   *Village Life in Northern India*. Urbana, University of Illinois Press.

Martin, J. W.
   1967   "The Cost of Parliamentary Enclosure in Warwickshire," in *Agriculture and Economic Growth in England 1650-1815*, ed. E. L. Jones. London, Methuen.

Mellor, J. W.
   1966   *The Economics of Agricultural Development*. Ithaca, Cornell University Press.

Moore, B., Jr.
   1966   *Social Origins of Dictatorship and Democracy*. Boston, Beacon Press.

Myrdal, G.
   1968   *Asian Drama*. New York, Random House.

Nobufumi, K.
   1964   The Characteristics of Heavy Application of Fertilizer in Japanese Agriculture. *The Developing Economies*, vol. 2, no. 4.

Ouchi, T.
   1966   The Japanese Land Reform, Its Efficiency and Limitations. *The Developing Economies,* vol. 4, no. 2.
Rosovsky, H.
   1968   Rumbles in the Rice Fields: Professor Nakamura vs. the Official Statistics. *The Journal of Asian Studies,* vol. 27, no. 2.
Smith, T. C.
   1959   *The Agrarian Origins of Modern Japan.* Stanford, Stanford University Press.
Tate, W. E.
   1967   *The English Village Community and the Enclosure Movements.* London, Victor Gollancz.
Warriner, D.
   1964   *Economics of Peasant Farming.* London, Frank Cass.
Wiser, W. H. and Wiser, C. V.
   1963   *Behind Mud Walls, 1930-1960.* Berkeley, University of California Press.

DAVID BURLESON

Caudill, William
   1953   "Applied Anthropology in Medicine," in *Anthropology Today,* ed. by A. L. Kroeber. Chicago, University of Chicago Press.
Dubos, Rene
   1959   *Mirage of Health,* New York, Doubleday.
Erasmus, Charles J.
   1961   *Man Takes Control,* Minneapolis, Bobbs-Merrill.
Ewell, Raymond
   1964   "Famine and Fertilizer," *Chemical Engineering News,* December, 14, 1964, pp. 106-117.
Garst, Jonathan
   1963   *No Need for Hunger,* New York, Random House.
Gonzales Casanova, Pablo
   1964   "Mexico Looks to the Future; The Need for Democracy." *The Atlantic,* March.
Moseman, Albert H.
   1964   *Agricultural Sciences For the Developing Nations,* American Academy for the Advancement of Science, Washington, D.C.
Polgar, Steven
   1962   "Health and Human Behavior," in *Current Anthropology,* Vol. 3, No. 7.

Redfield, Robert
1953   *The Primitive World and Its Transformations,* Ithaca, Cornell
        University Press.

Mary Helms

Casagrande, Joseph B.
1959   "Some observations on the study of intermediate societies," *In-
        termediate Societies, Social Mobility, and Communication,* V. F.
        Ray, ed. Proceedings of the 1959 Annual spring meeting of the
        American Ethnological Society. Seattle, University of Washington.

Foster, George M.
1967   "Introduction: What is a Peasant," in *Peasant Society: a Reader.*
        Jack M. Potter, May N. Diaz, George M. Foster, eds. Boston,
        Little, Brown and Co.

Halpern, Joel M. and John Brode
1967   "Peasant society: economic changes and revolutionary transforma-
        tion," In Bernard J. Siegel and Alan R. Beals, eds., *Biennial Re-
        view of Anthropology, 1967.* Stanford, Stanford University Press.

Helms, Mary W.
1967   *Frontier Society: Life in a Miskito Village in Eastern Nicaragua.*
        Ph.D. dissertation. Ann Arbor, Michigan, University Microfilms.

Izikowitz, Karl G.
1951   Lamet: Hill Peasants in French Indochina. *Ethnologiska Studier
        No. 17.* Goteborg, Sweden.

Leacock, Eleanor
1954   The Montagnais "hunting territory" and the fur trade. *American
        Anthropological Association, Memoir 78.*

Lehman, Frederick K.
1963   The Structure of Chin society. *Illinois Studies in Anthropology
        No. 3.* Urbana, University of Illinois Press.

Murphy, Robert
1960   *Headhunters Heritage.* Berkeley, University of California Press.

Murphy, Robert and Julian Steward
1956   Tappers and trappers: parallel process in acculturation. *Economic
        Development and Cultural Change* 4:335-355.

Redfield, Robert
1953   *The Primitive World and its Transformations.* Ithaca, Cornell
        University Press.
1956   *Peasant Society and Culture.* Chicago, University of Chicago Press.

Vanstone, James W.
　1962　*Point Hope, An Eskimo Village in Transition.* Seattle, University of Washington Press.
　1965　*The Changing Culture of the Snowdrift Chipewyan.* Bulletin No. 29. Ottawa, National Museum of Canada.
Wagley, Charles and Eduardo Galvao
　1949　*The Tenetehara of Brazil, a Culture in Transition.* New York, Columbia University Press.
Wolf, Eric R.
　1966　*Peasants.* Englewood Cliffs, N.J., Prentice-Hall, Inc.

E. A. Hammel

Adams, John Clinton
　1949　"Serbia in the first World War," in Robert J. Kerner, ed., *Yugoslavia.* Berkeley and Los Angeles: University of California Press.
Benedict, Burton
　1968　Family firms and economic development. *Southwestern Journal of Anthropology* 24:1-19.
Coon, Carleton S.
　1950　The mountains of giants; a racial and cultural study of the north Albanian mountain Ghegs. Papers of the Peabody Museum of American Archaeology and Ethnology 23(3). Cambridge: Harvard University Press.
Friedrich, Paul
　1962　An evolutionary sketch of Russian kinship. Proceedings of the 1962 Spring Meeting of the American Ethnological Society. Seattle: University of Washington Press.
Halpern, Joel M.
　1965　Peasant culture and urbanization in Yugoslavia. *Human Organization* 24:162-174.
Halpern, Joel M. and David Anderson
　MS　The zadruga: a century of change.
Halpern, Joel M. and E. A. Hammel
　MS　Observations on the intellectual history of the social sciences in Yugoslavia.
Hammel, E. A.
　1957　Serbo-Croatian kinship terminology. Papers of the Kroeber Anthropological Society 16:45-75. Berkeley.
　MSa　*Alternative Social Structures and Ritual Relations in the Balkans.* Englewood Cliffs: Prentice Hall (in press).
　MSb　The pink yo-yo: occupational mobility in Belgrade ca. 1915-1965.

Hoffman, George W. and Fred Warner Neal
1962   *Yugoslavia and The New Communism.* New York: Twentieth Century Fund.

Kostic, Cvetko
1955   Seljaci industriski radnici. Belgrade: Rad.
1959   Peasant industrial workers in Yugoslavia. *Man in India* 39:221-234.

Livada, Svetozar
1966   Staračka poljoprivredna domacinstva. *Sociologija Sela* 13-14:3-16. Zagreb: Agrarni Institut.

Lounsbury, Floyd G.
1964   "The formal analysis of Crow- and Omaha-type kinship terminologies," in Ward H. Goodenough, ed., *Explorations in Cultural Anthropology,* pp. 351-394. New York: McGraw Hill.

Magner, Thomas F.
1967   Language and nationalism in Yugoslavia. *Canadian Slavic Studies* 1:333-347.

Mosely, P. E.
1940   "The peasant family: the zadruga or communal joint-family in the Balkans and its recent evolution." In Caroline F. Ware, ed., *The Cultural Approach to History,* pp. 95-108. New York: Columbia University Press.
1943   Adaptation for survival: the Varžic zadruga. *Slavonic and East European Review* 21:147-173.
1953   The distribution of the zadruga within southeastern Europe. The Joshua Starr memorial volume, *Jewish Social Studies* 5:219-250.

Murphy, R. F. and L. Kasdan
1959   The structure of parallel cousin marriage. *American Anthropologist* 61:17-29.

Nader, Laura
1962   A note on attitudes and the use of language. *Anthropological Linguistics,* June, 1962, pp. 24-29.

Sahlins, Marshall
1961   The segmentary lineage: an organization of predatory expansion. *American Anthropologist* 63:322-345.

Sentic, M. and S. Obradovic
1963   Novi izvori za izučavanje migracije. *Stanovništvo* 1:305-314. Belgrade.

Socialistička Federativna Republika Jogoslavija (SFRJ)
1948   Popis stanovništva. Belgrade: Savezni Zavod za Statistiku.
1961   Popis stanovništva. Belgrade: Savezni Zavod za Statistiku.
1965   Statistički godišnjak. Belgrade: savezni Zavod za Statistiku.

Tomasic, Dinko
    1948   *Personality and Culture in Eastern European Politics.* New York: George W. Stewart.

ALEX WEINGROD

Bailey, F. G.
    1963   *Politics and Social Change.* Berkeley: University of California Press.

Barnouw and Krishnaswamy
    1963   *Indian Film.* New York: Columbia University Press.

Eliot, T. S.
    1949   *Notes Towards a Definition of Culture.* New York: Harcourt Brace.

Friedl, Ernestine
    1964   Lagging Emulation in Post Peasant Society. *American Anthropologist* 66:569-587.

Geertz, Clifford
    1962   Studies in Peasant Life: Community and Society. *Biennial Review of Anthropology, 1962,* B. Siegel, ed. Stanford: Stanford University Press.

Gough, Kathleen
    1965   Village Politics in Kerala-I. *The Economic Weekly,* Feb. 20:363-372.

Mayer, Adrian
    1966   "The Significance of Quasi-Groups in the Study of Complex Societies," in *The Social Anthropology of Complex Societies.* New York: Frederick A. Praeger.

Singer, Milton
    1959   "The Great Tradition in a Metropolitan Center: Madras," in *Traditional India: Structure and Change,* M. Singer, ed. Philadelphia: American Historical Society.

Weiner, Myron
    1957   *Party Politics in India.* Princeton: Princeton University Press.
    1964   *India's Two Political Cultures,* in mimeo. Cambridge: MIT Press.

EVA HUNT & ROBERT HUNT

Aquirre Beltran, Gonzalo
    1967   *Regiones de Refugio.* Instituto Indigenista Interamericano Ediciones Especiales No. 46. Mexico.

Brandenburg, Frank
  1964   *The Making of Modern Mexico.* Englewood Cliffs, New Jersey. Prentice-Hall, Inc.

Black, Mary and Duane Metzger
  1965   Ethnographic Description and the Study of Law. *American Anthropologist,* Special Issue: The Ethnography of Law. Vol. 67 (6):141-165.

Blau, Peter M.
  1955   *The Dynamics of Bureaucracy.* Chicago, University of Chicago Press.

Bohannan, Paul J.
  1965   The Differing Realms of the Law. *American Anthropologist,* The Ethnography of Law. Special Issue: Vol. 67 (6):33-42.

Deschamps Blanco, Rafael
  1958   *El Juicio de Amparo como Medio Indirecto de Control del Sistema Federal.* Mexico.

Echánove Trujillo, Carlos A.
  1949   La procédure Mexicaine d'Amparo. *Review Internationale de Droit Comparé,* III:229-248.

Gonzales Casanova, Pablo
  1965   *La Democracia en Mexico.* Mexico, Ediciones Era S.A.

Hunt, Robert C.
  1965   "The Developmental Cycle of the Family business in Rural Mexico," in *Essays in Economic Anthropology.* Proceedings of the American Ethnological Society. Seattle, University of Washington Press.
  1968   Agentes culturales Mestizos: establidad y cambio en Oaxaca. *América Indígena* (in press).

Hunt, Robert and Eva Hunt
  1967   Education as an interface institution in rural Mexico and the American Inner City. *Midway Magazine,* VIII, 2:99-109.

Lambert, Jacques
  1963   *Amèrique Latine: Structures Sociales et Institutions Politiques.* Presses Universitaires de France.

León Orantes, Romeo
  1951   *El Juicio de Amparo.* Mexico.

Leyes y Códigos de Mexico
  1964   Código Penal. Coleccion Porrúa. Mexico, Editorial Porrúa, S. A.

Metzger, Duane
  1960   Conflict in Chulsanto: A Village in Chiapas. *Alpha Kappa Deltan* 30:35-48.

Nader, Laura
  1964a   *Talea and Juquila: A Comparison of Social Organization.* University of California Publication in American Arch. and Ethnology. Vol. 48 (3).
  1964b   An Analysis of Zapotec Law Cases. *Ethnology* III (4):404-419.
  1965   Choices in Legal Procedure: Shia Moslem and Mexican Zapotec. *American Anthropologist,* 62(2):394-399.
  1966   "Variations in Rincon Zapotec Legal Procedure." In *Homenaje al Ingeniero Roberto Weitlaner.* Mexico. INAH. pp. 375-383.

Nader, Laura and Duane Metzger
  1963   Conflict Resolution in Two Mexican Communities: *American Anthropologist,* 65:584-592.

Nash, Manning
  1957   The Multiple Society in economic development: Mexico and Guatemala. *American Anthropologist,* 59:825-833.

Padgett, Vincent L.
  1966   *The Mexican Political System.* Boston, Houghton Mifflin Co.

Scott, Robert E.
  1964   *Mexican Government in Transition.* Urbana, University of Illinois Press.

Siegel, Sidney
  1956   *Nonparametric Statistics for the Behavioral Sciences.* New York, McGraw-Hill.

Stern, Lilo
  1966   *Kinship and Community in Chiapilla.* Unpublished Ph.D. dissertation submitted in the University of Cambridge, England.

Steward, Julian H.
  1950   *Area Research: Theory and Practice.* Soc. Sci. Research Council. Bulletin #63. New York.

Wolf, Eric
  1956   Aspects of group relations in a complex society: Mexico. *American Anthropologist,* 58:1065-1078.
  1966   *Peasants.* Englewood Cliffs, New Jersey, Prentice-Hall.

EDWARD P. DOZIER

Adams, Eleanor B. and Fray Angelico Chavez (eds.)
  1956   *The Missions of New Mexico, 1776.* Albuquerque. University of New Mexico Press.

Armstrong, John M.
  1949   *A Mexican Community: a Study of the Cultural Determinants of Migration.* Ph.D. dissertation, New Haven, Yale University.

Beals, Ralph L.
　1946　*Cheran: A Sierra Tarascan Village*. Washington, Smithsonian Institution, Institute of Social Anthropology, Publication No. 2.

Beals, Ralph L. and Norman D. Humphrey
　1957　*No Frontier to Learning: The Mexican Student in the United States*. Minneapolis, University of Minnesota Press.

Beegle, J. Allan, Harold F. Goldsmith, and Charles P. Loomis
　1960　Demographic characteristics of the United States-Mexican Border. *Rural Sociology* 25: 107-162.

Burma, John H.
　1949　The present status of Spanish Americans in New Mexico. *Social Forces* 28:133-38.
　1954　*Spanish-speaking Groups in the United States*. Durham, Duke University Press.

Campa, Arthur
　1932　Religious Spanish folk-drama. *New Mexico Quarterly* 2.

Chavez, Manuel (Fray Angelico)
　1954　The penitentes of New Mexico. *New Mexico Historical Review*, 29:97-123.

Clark, Margaret
　1959　*Health in the Mexican-American Culture*. Berkeley and Los Angeles, University of California Press.

Edmonson, Munro S.
　1957　*Los Manitos: A Study of Institutional Values*. Tulane University of Louisiana. Middle American Research Institute. Publication No. 25, Pt. 1, New Orleans.

Fergusson, Erna
　1951　*New Mexico: A Pageant of Three Peoples*. New York, Alfred A. Knopf.

Foster, George
　1951　Report on an ethnological reconnaissance of Spain. *American Anthropologist* 53:311-325.
　1953a　What is folk culture? *American Anthropologist* 55:159-173.
　1953b　Cofradia and compadrazgo in Spain and Spanish America. *Southwestern Journal of Anthropology* 9:1-28.
　1960　*Culture and Conquest: America's Spanish Heritage*. Viking Fund, Publication on Anthropology No. 27. New York, Wenner-Gren Foundation for Anthropological Research, Inc.
　1961　The dyadic contract: a model for the social structure of a Mexican peasant village. *American Anthropologist* 63:1173-92.
　1962　*Traditional Cultures and the Impact of Technological Change*. New York, Harper.

1963   The dyadic contract in Tzintzuntzan, II: patron-client relationships. *American Anthropologist* 65:1280-94.

Francis, E. K.
1956   Padre Martinez: A New Mexican myth. *New Mexico Historical Review* 31:265-289.

Gamio, Manuel
1930   *Mexican Immigration to the United States*. Chicago, University of Chicago Press.

Getty, Harry
1949   Unpublished manuscript. In author's possession.

Gillin, John.
1947   Modern Latin-American culture. *Social Forces* 25:243-248.

Hammond, G. P.
1926   Don Juan de Oñate, and the founding of New Mexico. *New Mexico Historical Review* 1:42-77; 2:156-92.

Hawley, Florence and Donovan Senter
1946   Group designed behavior patterns in two acculturating groups. *Southwestern Journal of Anthropology* 2:133-151.

Haynes, N. S.
1954   The family in Mexico. *Marriage and Family Living* 16:369-373.

Hewes, Gordon
1954   Mexicans in search of the Mexican. *American Journal of Economics and Sociology* 13:209-223.

Holland, William R.
1963   Mexican-American medical beliefs: science or magic. *Arizona Medicine* 20:89-101.

Iturriaga, Jose
1951   *La estructura social y cultural de Mexico*. Mexico City, Fondo de Cultura Economica.

Kluckhohn, Florence and Fred L. Strodtbeck
1961   *Variations in Value Orientations*. Evanston. Row, Peterson and Company.

Kroeber, Alfred L.
1948   *Anthropology*. New York, Harcourt-Brace.

Kurath, Gertrude
1949   Mexican moriascas. *Journal of American Folklore* 62:87-106.

Landman, Ruth
1963   *Some Aspects of the Acculturation of Mexican Immigrants and Descendants to American Culture*. Ph.D. dissertation, New Haven, Yale University.

Leonard, Olen and Loomis, Charles P.
  1941 *Culture of a Contemporary Rural Community: El Canito, New Mexico.* Department of Agriculture, Bureau of Agricultural Economics, Rural Life Studies, No. 1. Washington, Government Printing Press.

Lewis, Oscar
  1949 Husbands and wives in a Mexican village: a study of role conflict. *American Anthropologist* 51:602-610.
  1951 *Life in a Mexican Village.* Urbana, University of Illinois Press.
  1952 Urbanization without breakdown: a case study. *The Scientific Monthly* 75:31-41.

Madsen, William
  1961 *Society and Health in the Lower Rio Grande Valley.* Hogg Foundation for Mental Health. Austin, The University of Texas.
  1964 *The Mexican-Americans of South Texas.* New York: Holt, Rinehart and Winston.

McWilliams, Carey
  1945 *Brothers under the Skin.* Boston, Little, Brown & Company.

Mintz, Sidney W. and Wolf, Eric R.
  1950 An analysis of ritual co-parenthood (Compadrazgo). *Southwestern Journal of Anthropology* 6:341-368.

Owen, Roger C.
  1959 *Morabavi: A Study of an Assimilated Group in Northern Sonora.* Tucson, Anthropological Papers of The University of Arizona, No. 3.

Parsons, Elsie Clews
  1936 *Mitla: Town of the Souls.* Chicago, University of Chicago Press.

Paz, Octavio
  1947 *El laberinto de la soledad.* Cuadernos Americanos 16, Mexico.

Pineda, Francisco Gonzalez
  1959 *El Mexicano, sudinámica psicosocial.* Monografias psicoanaliticas No. 2, Asociacion Psicoanalitica Mexicana, A. C.

Ramirez, S.
  1959 *El Mexicano, psicologia de sus motivaciones.* Monografias psicoanaliticos No. 1, Asociacion Psicoanalitica Mexicana, A.C.

Ramirez, S. and R. Parres
  1957 Some dynamic factors in the organization of the Mexican family. *International Journal of Social Psychiatry* 3:18-21.

Ramos, Samuel
  1962 *Profile of Man and Culture in Mexico.* Austin, University of Texas Press.

Redfield, Robert
    1930   *Tepoztlan*. Chicago, University of Chicago Press.
    1956   *Peasant Society and Culture: An Anthropological Approach to Civilization*. Chicago, University of Chicago Press.

Romano, Actavio Ignacio
    1960   Donship in a Mexican-American community in Texas. *American Anthropologist* 62:966-976.
    n.d.   Charismatic Medicine, folk-healing and folk-sainthood. Manuscript accepted for publication, *American Anthropologist*.

Ross, William T.
    1953   *Social Functions of the Mexican-American Godparent System in Tucson*. M.A. thesis, Tucson, University of Arizona.

Sanchez, George I.
    1940   *Forgotten People: A Study of New Mexicans*. Albuquerque, University of New Mexico Press.

Sandoval, Tomas Cordova
    1951   Indios, criollos y mestizos. *Cuadernos Americanos* 3, Mexico.

Saunders, Lyle
    1954   *Cultural Differences and Medical Care*. New York, Russel Sage Foundation.

Scholes, France V.
    1935   Civil government and society in the seventeenth century. *New Mexico Historical Review* 10:71-111.

Simpson, Eyler N.
    1937   *The Ejido: Mexico's Way Out*. Chapel Hill, University of North Carolina Press.

Spicer, Edward H.
    1940   *Pascua: a Yaqui Village in Arizona*. Chicago, University of Chicago Press.
    1954   *Potam: A Yaqui Village in Sonora*. Memoirs of the American Anthropological Association, No. 77.

Stanislawski, Dan
    1947   Early town planning in the new world. *The Geographical Review* 37:95-105.

Stoker, David H.
    1963   *A Comparison of the Symptomatic Behavior of Spanish-American and Anglo-American Hospital Patients*. M.A. thesis, Tucson, Department of Psychology, University of Arizona.

Tuck, Ruth D.
    1946   *Not With the Fist: Mexican Americans in a Southwest City*. New York, Harcourt, Brace and Company.

Tucson Project Statement
   1960   Research proposal statement made to the U.S. Department of
           Health, Education, and Welfare, Washington, D.C. Grant No.
           2RC-580(240). Copy filed in Department of Psychology, The Uni-
           versity of Arizona, Tucson.

Twitchell, Ralph E.
   1909   *History of the Military Occupation of the Territory of New
           Mexico from 1846 to 1851.* Denver, Smith-Brooks Company.

United States Department of Agriculture, Soil Conservation Service
   1935   *Tewa Basin Study, volume II: The Spanish-American villages.*
           Albuquerque, Economic Surveys Division.

Uranga, Emilio
   1949   Ensayo de una ontoloqia del Mexicano. *Cuadernos Americanos* 2.

United States Bureau of the Census
   1963   U.S. Census Population: 1960, Subject Reports. Persons of Spanish
           Surname. Final Report PC(2)-1B. U.S. Government Printing Office,
           Washington, D.C.

Wagley, Charles and Marvin Harris
   1955   A typology of Latin American subcultures. *American Anthro-
           pologist* 57:428-451.

Whetten, Nathan C.
   1948   *Rural Mexico.* Chicago, University of Chicago Press.

Wolf, Eric R.
   1955   Types of Latin American peasantry: a preliminary discussion.
           American Anthropologist 57:452-471.